LOCAL GOVERNMENT ADMINISTRATION IN PRACTICE IN SOUTH SUDAN

JUSTICE EQUALITY DIGNITY

DR. ANEI MANGONG ANEI NGONG

A Note from the Publisher

The publisher wishes to acknowledge and thank Dr Douglas H. Johnson for his invaluable help and support for Africa World Books and its mission of preserving and promoting African cultural and literary traditions and history. Dr Johnson and fellow historians have been instrumental in ensuring that African people remain connected to their past and their identity. Africa World Books is proud to carry on this mission.

Africa
World Books
Pty Ltd

DEDICATION

To the Marginalized Grassroots
of the Republic of South Sudan.

CONTENTS

Chapter Six: The Civil Service Of The Local Government Council in South Sudan   153

Tables and Figures

ACKNOWLEDGMENTS

I would like to give my profound gratitude and thanks to Professor Dr. Abraham Matoc Dhal for having certified my work as worthy for publication as a book and also for having written a forward for my book.

I owe thanks to my interviewees: Mr. Del Rumdit Deng, Executive Director of Local Government Board; Mr. Marko Mabior Ajiec, Executive Director of Tonj South County; Mr. Abun Deng, Inspector of Local Government, Tonj South County; Mr. Gabriel Majok Manyual, Chairman, Tonj South County Council; Mr. Diing Aleu Diing, Inspector of Local Government, Tonj Municipality; Mr. Natale Nhial Deng, Chief Executive Officer, Tonj Municipality; Mr. Athuai Mangong Manyuon, Deputy Director of Accounts, Tonj Municipality; Hon. Madhang Majok Meen, Former Governor of Gok State; Hon. Tombura Jal Tut, Former Minister of Agriculture, Forestry, Fisheries and Live Stock, Latjor State; Hon. Job Alawei Magot, former Commissioner of Aweirial County of Eastern Lakes State. All of them provided valuable information which enabled me to compile this book.

I'm also indebted to Hon. Clement Khamis Kamoyangi, Chairperson of the Local Government Board, and Mr. Malony Akau Nai for having availed for me the information on the Presidential Orders for the Creation of the New States (28 & 32 states) and their Counties.

I give thanks to my son Makoc, student in the College of Medicine, University of Juba, for having assisted me to key board some tables of this book.

My thanks also go to Dr. Tong Chor Malek, Secretary General, South Sudan National Olympics Committee and Mr. Ariik Machar, Office Manager of the Minister of Justice and Constitutional Development for having assisted me to print a copy of the manuscript of this book.

Lastly but not least, I owe thanks to Lecturer Joseph Lual Dario Deng who made the table of contents and prepared the book in the programme of publishers.

FORWARD

All over the world, a country without sound, efficient and effective Local Government Administration in practice hardly develops nor achieves substantial sustainable economic growth or development. In particular developing countries like Republic of South Sudan pre-requisites is the practical application of the Local Government Administration succinctly narrated in this book.

Impressively the book set out a number of basic well thought out objectives of local government administration such as being an instrument of decentralization, democracy, freedom, method of achieving administrative efficiency and a means of attaining economic development. These objectives are so inspiring and they make the book to be an invaluable document to read with much concern.

Moreover, the author has used relevant literature and has comprehensively made sufficient comparison of local government administration such as taking UK, Sudan as well as examining the situation as it exists in the Republic of South Sudan. Indeed, the book is enjoyable to read and it is worthy for practical application in our country.

The policy makers, administrators, teaching staff in the universities, particularly specialists in public administration, governance and local government administrators, students doing public administration and local government, researchers and the public will surely find answers to local government problems which exist practically in the country.

Finally, the study is exceptionally a good answer to practical implications and complexities of local government administration in a decentralized developing country like the South Sudan. Also, it is importantly crucial to read the book thoroughly to enable you to reap the benefits of local government administration.

Prof. Abraham Matoc Dhal (Ph.D.)
Vice Chancellor,
Dr. John Garang Memorial University of Science and Technology, Bor.

PREFACE

The purpose of this book is to avail information on local government to the elites, academicians, scholars, researchers and students of the country and any others who could benefit from this book particularly the practitioners of the local government in the Republic of South Sudan. The book can serve as a reference to those who are interested to have more perspective and knowledge about the local government.

The book covers the general framework of local government and the way it is being applied worldwide; and with how local government is being practiced or applied in the Republic of South Sudan.

In the Republic of South Sudan, the Government had enshrined in the Constitution decentralization as the system of governance in the country. But in actual fact, the government is for recentralization system of governance which in away is a paradox.

All the provisions of Local Government Act, 2009 have not been followed accurately. There is lack behind in the implementation of the Local Government Act, 2009. For example, even if the councils are nominated by their constituencies, they are not involved in decision making. It is either the state governments or the commissioners who take unilateral decisions without consultation with the councilors. The departments established in the counties are mostly accountable to their states' departments and do not provide adequate services to the grass roots. Warrants for the establishment of local councils whether at County or Payam levels have not been issued.

Some parts of the criteria for the establishment of a county are not fulfilled as prescribed by the LGA 2009. The organs of the councils (legislature, executive and customary law) exist by name in the LGA 2009 but are not operational even if they are formed. The councils are not exercising the responsibilities prescribed in the LGA 2009.

No services being rendered by the local government councils. Some NGOs and others render some services in the fields of health, agriculture, relief, water and education.

Local councils do not collect much revenue from sources of revenue generation besides Social Service Tax, Court Fees and Fines, market fees and auction fees. Councils depend much on grant-in-aid from the national government.

Although the Local Government Board is trying its best to promote the well being of local government institutions in the country, the fact that its functions and powers are limited to review and formulation of local government policies as well as recommendation and coordination of the establishment of minimum standards and uniform norms for service delivery makes it not much effective in enforcing the implementation of the Local Government Act.

It is explicit that in the Republic of South Sudan there is no conviction to law, and it is what is making the implementation of Local Government Act to be disregarded by the national and states' leaderships, which brought the failure of both governments to provide adequate service delivery to the rural populace.

ABBREVIATIONS

BDCs Boma Development Committees
CACs Community Accountability Committees
CANS Civil Authority of New Sudan
CDG County Development Grant
CEPO Community Empowerment Organization
CLCs County Local Councils
CMAs Civil Military Administrators
CMOs Civil Military Officers
CPA Comprehensive Peace Agreement
COVID-19 Corona Virus Infectious Disease
CTMCs County Transfers Monitoring Committees
ESMF Environment and Social Management Framework
EU European Union
FY Financial Year/Fiscal Year
GATC Government Accountancy Training Centre
GEAR Growth Employment and Redistribution
GIZ German Development Cooperation
GoSS Government of Southern Sudan
GRM Grievance Redress Mechanism

GRSS Government of the Republic of South Sudan
GTT Grant-Tracking Tool
HRD Human Resources Development
ICSS Interim Constitution of South Sudan
ICT Information Communication Technology
JPA Joint Plan of Action
KMIS Knowledge Management Information System
LGA Local Government Act
LGAO Local Government Administrative Officer
LGAOs Local Government Administrative Officers
LGB Local Government Board
LG Local Government
LGOs Local Government Officers
LOGOSEED Local Governance and Service Delivery Project
LGs Local Governments
LSS Local Service Support
M&E Monitoring & Evaluation
MoFEP Ministry of Finance and Economic Planning
MoPS&HRD Ministry of Public Service and Human Resource
Development
NGOs Non Governmental Organizations
OJT On-the-Job Training (OJT)
PC Provincial Commissioner
PDCs Payam Development Committees
PDG Payam Development Grant
PDGs Payam Development Grants
PDG Payam Development Grant
PEC Provincial Executive Council
PFM Public Financial Management
PHCC Primary Health Care Centre

PHCU Primary Health Care Units
PMC Project Management Committee
PM&E Project Monitoring and Evaluation
PMU Project Monitoring Unit
PRS Panchayati Raj System
RSS Republic of South Sudan
SMART Specific, Measureable, Attainable, Realistic and Time bound
SMoLG State Ministry of Local Government
SPLA/M Sudan People's Liberation Army/Movement
SSDP South Sudan Development Plan
SRA Sudan Relief Association
SSU Sudanese Socialist Union
SSRF South Sudan Recovery Fund
ToTs Training of Trainers
TUWSS Torit Urban Water Supply and Sanitation Services Ltd.
TWGs Technical Working Groups
UN United Nations
UNDP United Nations Development Programme
UNMISS United Nations Mission in South Sudan
USAID United States of America Aid
USD United States Dollar
WWS Within and Without the State
YTWSS Yei Town Water and Sanitation Services Ltd.
YUWASO Yambio Urban Water and Sanitation Services Company Ltd.

CHAPTER ONE

LOCAL GOVERNMENT ADMINISTRATION

1.1 Introduction

Local government is a form of public administration which in a majority of contexts, exists as the lowest tier of administration within a given state. The term is used to contrast with offices at state level, which are referred to as the central government, national government, or where appropriate federal government and also to supranational government which deals with governing institutions between states. Local governments generally act within powers delegated to them by legislation or directives of the higher level of government. In federal states, local government generally comprises the third or sometimes the fourth tier of government, whereas in unitary states, local government usually occupies the second or third tier of government, often with greater powers than higher-level administrative divisions.

The issue of municipal autonomy is a key question of public administration and governance. The institutions of local government vary greatly between countries, and even where similar arrangements exist, the terminology often varies. Common names for local government entities include state, province, region, department, county, prefecture, district, city, township, town, borough, parish, municipality, shire, village, and local service district.[1] In South Sudan local government institutions include county, municipality, town, Payam and Boma.

Local government administration occurs at the city, borough, and district, municipal or county level and is the operation of government closest to where people live. Local governments have specific local powers and functions not covered by other levels of government, and local administrators are elected by the local population.[2] Whereas in South Sudan, Local Government Administrative Officers (LGAOs) are appointed civil servants.

Local government is an administrative body for a small geographic area, such as a city, town, county, or state. A local government will typically only have control over their specific geographical region, and cannot pass or enforce laws that will affect a wider area.

Because of the role local authorities' play, the range of matters for which they are responsible and their closeness to local communities, local government has a more immediate effect on the day-to-day lives of the people than most other sectors of public administration. Local government has, therefore, both a representational and an operational role, with responsibility for a range of services.

Local government is a form of public administration which in a majority of contexts, exists as the lowest tier of administration within a given state.

---

1   From Wikipedia, the free encyclopedia
2   Define Local Government Administration, By J-Jeffrey, eHow Contributor.

Local government is the public administration of towns, cities, counties and districts. Municipal government is the public administration of a township, village, borough, city or town. Municipalities have municipal ordinances, which are laws, rules or regulations made and enforced by a city government. Most states have at least two tiers of local government: counties and municipalities. In some states, counties are divided into townships. In the case of South Sudan, local government has three tiers "County/Municipality, Payam/Block and Boma/Quarter". There are several different types of jurisdictions at the municipal level, including the city, town, borough, and village.

Of course, people expect state and local governments to provide services such as police protection, education, highway building and maintenance, welfare programmes, and hospital and health care. Taxes are a major source of income to pay for these services and many others that hit close to home.

The existence of local government has always been defended on the basis that it is a crucial aspect of the process of democratization and intensification of mass participation in the decision-making process. No political system is considered complete and democratic if it does not have a system of local government.

The legal character of a local authority thus comprises two elements, the elected council of the authority and the chief executive, with responsibility for performing local authority functions shared between them. However, legally all functions, whether performed by the elected council or by the chief executive, are exercised on behalf of the local authority.[3]

The existence of local government has always been defended on the basis that it is a crucial aspect of the process of democratization

---

3   Putting People First An Action Programme for Effective Local Government.

and intensification of mass participation in the decision making process. No political system is considered complete and democratic if it does not have a system of local government.

1.2. Conceptualization of Local Government

The term 'Local government' is an elusive one, not least because most people comfortably assume they understand what it is. But in fact, it can mean different things to different people. For an Englishman for example, it is likely to mean 'the Council', which may perform any number of tasks from cutting grass and collecting rates, to establishing new secondary schools. More to the point, the English 'Council' is a local body which is broadly accepted by local people and which possesses a substantial measure of authority independent of the central government in London. For a rural Sudanese, on the other hand, the local government council may be seen as simply 'the Government" or *el Hakuma*. It may also concern itself with tidying up streets and collecting taxes and even establishing schools, but this is often regarded as the work not of a local body but of the field administrators or representatives of the central ministries (of Education, Works, etc. as well as of Local Government) in Khartoum.[4]

In many states, particularly in Africa, the concept of local government is confusing because of the past colonial administrative strategies with the shifting strategies of different post-colonial elites, and also with uncertain attempts at creating development-orientated administrative structures. In the process, some authors would consider the term 'local administration' has become preferable to 'local government', given the increasing centralized power in most

---

4   John Howell (Ed.). <u>Local Government and Politics in the Sudan</u>. Khartoum, Sudan, Khartoum Printing Press, 1974, P. 1.

new states.[5]

According to the United Nations Division of Public Administration, 'local government is a political division of a nation either federal system, or a state which is constituted by law and has substantial control of local affairs, including the powers to impose taxes or exact labour for prescribed purposes. The governing body of such an entity is elected or otherwise locally selected (Ola & Tonwe, 2003). It was also described by Whalen (1970) as the local unit of government in any system assumed to possess a given territory and population, an institutional structure, a separate legal identity, a range of powers and functions authorized by delegation from the appropriate central or intermediate legislature and lastly within the ambit of such delegation, autonomy subject always to the test of reasonableness. For example, local government in Nigeria is "Government at local levels exercised through representative councils established by law to exercise specific powers within defined areas. These powers should give the council substantial control over local affairs, including staffing, and institutional and financial powers to initiate and to determine and implement projects so as to compliment the activities of the state and federal government in their areas, and ensure through devolution of functions to those councils and through the active participation of the people and their traditional institutions, that local initiative and response to local needs and conditions are maximized" (FGN, 1976). To Maddick (1963), local governments can be viewed as sub-units of government controlled by a local council which is authorized by the central government to pass ordinances having local application, levy taxes or exact labour and within limit specified by the central government, vary centrally decided policies in local application.

---

5   Ibid. P. 1.

1.3. Definition of Local Government

The definition of Local Government differs from one country to the other. This is because the definition is determined by the sort of social services and goods which are expected to be provided by the state. Issues concerning industrialization, population growth, the problems of the communities living in the rural and urban areas, and the attitude of the ruling political system towards centralization and decentralization of power are all the factors that bring different approaches to local government in terms of definition, principles, structure and location.

It should not be expected that there could be similarity of local government system of one country with that of the other. This is because of the cultural, ecological, environmental, ideological and technological development differences between the countries over the world.

Basically, local government is a public organization which is entrusted with the formulation of policies and to decide on matters of policy interest within a geographical area. Local government has a general jurisdiction and is not confined to a specific function or service. Its area of jurisdiction may be divided into provinces, districts, quarter or village councils. For example, in South Sudan, Counties, Municipalities, Payams, Bomas, Blocks and Quarters are some kinds of Local Government units.

There are many definitions of local government and some are as below:

1. Local government is defined as the people who have the authority to make decisions or pass laws in a small geographic area near to them.[6] One example of local government is the town council.

---

6   Your Dictionary definition and usage example. Copyright © 2014 by Love To Know Corp

2. Local government is the "Government of the affairs of a town, district, etc. by the people living there."[7]

3. Local government is "Any form of government whose remit covers an area less than that of the nation and, in some cases, less than that of a state."[8]

4. Local government is "The government that controls and makes decisions for a local area (such as a town, city, or county), or the government of a specific local area constituting a subdivision of a major political unit (as a nation or state); also: the body of persons constituting such a government."[9]

5. Local government is "The administration of a particular town, county, or district, with representatives elected by those who live there."[10]

6. Local government is "The organization that provides public services in a particular town or area, controlled by officials chosen in local elections. 'It is the Government of the affairs of counties, towns, etc, by locally elected political bodies.'"[11]

7. For South Sudan, local government "means the level of government closest to the people within a State…as provided under Article 50 of the Constitution" (LGA, 2009, P. 4.).

There are other more definitions by other scholars as shall be found hereunder.

Local government is a product of devolution as a dimension of decentralization. Olowu (1988: 12) remarks:

---

7   Webster's New World College Dictionary Copyright © 2010 by Wiley Publishing, Inc., Cleveland, Ohio.

8   English Wiktionary.

9   Marriam-Webster, m-w.com, An Encyclopedia Britannica Company.

10   Britannica.com: Encyclopedia article about "local government."

11   Collins English Dictionary – Complete and Unabridged © HarperCollins Publishers 1991, 1994, 1998, 2000, 2003.

"There are two approaches to the definition of local government in the literature. One approach, which is usually adopted in comparative studies, is to regard all such national structures below the central government as local government. A second approach is more circumspect in that local governments are identified by certain defining characteristics. These characteristics usually focus on the following five attributes: legal personality, specified powers to perform a range of functions, substantial budgetary and staffing autonomy subject to limited central control, effective citizen participation and localness. These are regarded as essential to distinguish it from all other forms of local institutions and also ensure its organizational effectiveness."

These so called essential features of local government are misleading. Not all local governments provide an opportunity for effective citizen participation. There are various issues to be considered. A number of questions arise. How is effective citizen participation determined? Is it determined in terms of electoral participation? Is citizen participation unique to local government? With these issues in mind it appears that the same problems afflict identifying legal personality as a feature of local government, for legal personality is not a monopoly of local government.

However, Robson (1937: 574) defines local government from a legal point of view as:

"In general, local government may be said to involve the conception of a territorial, non-sovereign community possessing the legal right and the necessary organization to regulate its own affairs. This, in turn, presupposes the existence of a local authority with power to act independent of external control as well as the participation of the local community in the administration of its own affairs."

Whereas, Gomme (1987: 1-2) defines local government in the following manner:

"Local government is that part of the whole government of a nation or state which is administered by authorities subordinate to the state authority, but elected independently of control by the state authority, by qualified persons resident, or having property in certain localities, which localities have been formed by communities having common interests and common history."

While, Meyer (1978: 10) defines local government as follows:

"Local democratic governing units within the unitary democratic system of a country which are subordinate members of the government vested with prescribed, controlled governmental powers and sources of income to render specific local services and to develop, control and regulate the geographic, social and economic environment of defined local area."

One could argue that the weakness of Meyer's definition is that it includes democracy as an essential element of local government whilst a local government can exist without being democratic in the same way that a national government can exist in a country without that government being democratic. For instance, a government brought into power through a coup de' etat may be called repressive and undemocratic. It is thus also possible to refer to an undemocratic local government. In spite of this weakness in Mayer's definition, it seems to capture the essence of local government, which is closely linked to the distinct characteristics indentified by Marshall. The essence is therefore, is that local government is a government institution with limited legislative power and author-ity, which operates within clearly defined geographical and legal jurisdiction, within a nation or state. The defining feature of local government is the authority to enact legislation within the defined jurisdiction and therefore the enjoyment of a measure of autonomy. These characteristics of local government should be considered with the restructuring of local government so as to ensure that the purpose of local government is not overlooked.

On the other hand, Marshall's (1965:1) definition seems to come closer to the real features of local government and identifies three distinct characteristics which are as follows:

"Operation in a restricted geographical area within a nation or state, local election or selection; and the enjoyment of a measure of autonomy."

1.4. Objectives of Local Government Administration

There are various reasons why governments establish local government administration. Some of these reasons are that: Local Government is considered as an instrument of decentralization; democracy; freedom; method of achieving administrative efficien-cy; and means of attaining economic development.

1. Local Government Administration as an instrument of decentralization: There are two main methods of decentraliza-tion: Deconcentration and Devolution. Deconcentration is done by an administrative order. Authority is delegated to lower levels of the central government organization.

Devolution is done through legal process of law. Devolution is divided in to two: Administrative devolution and Political devolu-tion. In administrative devolution powers are delegated to the local government administration. In political devolution, authority involves a great measure of political responsibility. It involves constitutional recognition. The 1972 Regional Autonomy for the Southern Region of the Sudan and the 2005 Government of Southern Sudan (GoSS) are examples of the political devolution of powers. Federation is also another example of political devolution.

Decentralization at times acts to improve national unity. It diffuses regional feelings. It makes the communities to look at the local authorities. It may push those who are in opposition of the central government to a position of association. People are given the opportunity to decide on how they should be ruled. It reduces friction.

2. Democracy: It is necessary to have elected representatives who participate in decision-making and running the affairs of the community. There are governments which want to improve their systems because of the idea of participation of citizens. This idea is what brought local government into the fore in other countries of the world, e.g. Britain, Canada, Denmark, Sweden and later Sudan.

3. Freedom: Freedom is the right of a citizen and also of the communities. Citizens need to be given a right to think in their own way and how to choose their way of living. Members of community are given freedom to live in the way they think good to themselves.

4. Efficiency of administration: Centralization does not allow services to reach citizens easily. Decisions made in the center are most likely to be irrelevant in the case of the peripheries. When units are created in the local areas they will be more efficient and effective. Breaking up a country into local units is necessary because the central government will not be able to answer all the problems in different areas.

5. Social and Economic Development: There are specific areas where local contribution is needed and given. Decisions at the center always demand local effort/contribution even if it means participation of local government in mobilizing local contribution. Local government institutions are always effective in instilling self-reliance.

1.5. Features of Local Government Administration

Generally, despite not having an agreement on the term, some features of local government that resonate are as the following:

i.   It is made up of democratically constituted representative council;

ii. it must exercise financial autonomy in taxable jurisdiction of local significance;

iii. it possesses functional autonomy in delivery of legally recognized services;

iv. it has autonomy in the recruitment of its staff;

v.   it must possess definite geographical territory; and

vi. should have local population, among others.

However, while these features are the habitual characteristics of local government in developed nations like Great Britain, France, United States of America, amongst others, it becomes a concern but sad reality that these features are near absent in the system of local government practiced in Africa particularly in Nigeria and South Sudan.

1.6. Relationships between Local Government and Central Government

Both Robson and Gomme seem to emphasize independence whilst local governments are actually not independent of central government control. Local governments enjoy only relative autonomy, due to the division of responsibilities for services between national and local government. It should be noted that the division of responsibilities is a political or policy issue.

There are several preconditions that determine successful relationships between central and local government as indicated by the World Bank (1989:88) and Heymans & Totemeyer (1988: 6). These preconditions are:

1. The need and urge for a strong system of local government in a democratic political environment.
2. That local government be allowed to play a vital role as a full partner in regional and national development.
3. A fair division of financial resources between central, regional and local bodies.
4. A fair division of human resources between central and local government.
5. Formal and effective checks and balances between central and local government.
6. Full and adequate consultation and a regular flow of accurate information at and between all levels.
7. The full participation of each citizen, irrespective of race and gender at all levels of administration and government-thus, the extension of democracy to all levels of government.
8. Political and social harmony.
9. Defined legal relations between the different levels of

government and the ability for local pressure on central government to change legislation.
10. Trust and honesty as basic principles of government.
11. Openness to innovation.

Local governments should be seen as the cornerstones in the structure of a democratic political system since local government serves as a vehicle for intelligent and responsible citizenship on this particular level.

1.7. Local Authority

A local authority, sometimes also referred to as a municipal authority, is a term that refers to a rural and urban political subdivision below the national level which is constituted by law and has a substantial control of local affairs, and which includes authorities in counties, municipalities, cities, villages and others. The term excludes district or regional subdivisions of the national government that are set up solely for national administrative purposes (United Nations, 1997: vi).

Local authorities are created to render services in defined geographical areas, primarily because of the inability of central government to attend in detail to all the requirements of society that have to be satisfied by a government institution. The range of urban services provided by local authorities in developing countries, more particularly in Africa, are *inter alia*, parks, street cleaning, sanitation, refuse collection, road construction and maintenance, housing, water and sewerage, primary education, clinics, residential and industrial estates, planning and zoning, fire and ambulance services, camping sites and recreational services (Meyer, 1978: 12).

A local authority is thus a public institution functioning under the direction and control of an elected council but subject to the directives of the national and provincial legislative and political executive institutions. A local authority is a corporate body which is a legal person and exists separately from and independently of the persons who head it. Local authorities are created to give residents of their area a say in the government and administration of local affairs and are vested with specific powers to enable them to make by-laws, which are not inconsistent with the legislation passed by Parliament and provincial legislatures. Local authorities are usually headed by councils consisting of elected members. In other words local authorities are intended to be democratic institutions which are responsive to real needs and the justifiable expectations of people. They are thus subject to public accountability and therefore, it is important to focus on local government democracy.

1.8. Criteria for Creation of Local Government Units

Local government creation in Nigeria has been through numerous experiences that we tend to ask at some points in time: "who creates local government?" Numerous attempts have been geared towards bringing government nearer to the people at the most basic level. The importance of bringing government nearer to the people cannot be overemphasized. This translates to bringing services of great importance to the welfare and livelihood of the community. Such services have high positive implication on the standard of living of the people at this primary level of administration.

1.8.1. Creation of Local Government Units

In some countries in Africa, local government units are established by state governments. States use their own constitutions to legalize and define their local governments. The states do that by passing ordinances, or regulations that follow state laws. For example, in Nigeria local government units are established by the States.

The Nigerian experience has brought another dimension to discourse of local government being a residual affair of the state government as it is obtainable in classic federal states like United States, Canada amongst others. In other words, creation of local government unit is the prerogative of a state, provincial or regional government. The Nigerian case through the local government creation tussle between the federal government and Lagos State government has left many wondering which level of government wields the power to create local government.[12]

Whereas in South Sudan although local government is under the state governments, the creation of local government units is as prescribed in the Local Government Act 2009, Section 20 (3): "Each Local Government Council shall be created and established by an order issued by the President upon the recommendation of the State Government."

1.8.2. Criteria for Creation of Local Government Units

The unceasing demand for creation of local government is not far-fetched and cannot be dissociated from the need to engender and stimulate grassroots development, improve the civic conscious-ness and local participation in local governance which serves as the foundation upon which democracy itself is built. Moreover, the need to decongest the national government and relieve national leaders of onerous details about grassroots governance is another call.

In view of this, certain criteria are pertinent to be considered in local government creation. These criteria are:

---

12   Mujeeb Muriana (2018), Who creates local government and what are the criteria for local government creation in Nigeria, Munich, GRIN Verlag, https://www.grin.com/document/962643.

i. **Population:** Local government being the closest level of government must have a reasonably small population. The population must not be too small or too large. The central idea herein is to foster closer relationship between the local populace with their government. For example, in Nigeria, the 1976 Local Government Reforms identified the benchmark figure as between 150,000 and 800,000. Some local governments in France and other developed countries have as low as twenty thousand as population.

ii. **Historical background:** The communities willing to form a local government area must necessarily possess a common historical background. This is to harness homogeneity of interest and preferences to avoid certain conflicts being preeminent in heterogeneous communities.

iii. **Social and cultural affinity:** The communities in question must also have social and cultural affinity with each other to ease governance among members and interest aggregation. The heterogeneity of identity and cultures of the locals should be as minimal as possible to avoid conflict of interest and sabotage governance.

iv. **Economic viability:** The central idea of viability lies in sustainability. That is, how realistically sustainable is the local government to be created going to be. In essence, the economic implication entails the issue of finance needed to run governance and its continuous availability. Finance is at the heart of governance and the ability of the local government to be created to raise a substantial part of its revenue is crucial therein.

v. **Predilection of the central or state government:** members of the council to be constituted are to be either directly elected by local populace or appointed by the federal or state government. In the contemporary context, Section **7** (1) of the 1999 Constitution of the Federal Republic of Nigeria (2011 as amended) states that 'the system of local government by democratically elected local government councils is under this Constitution guaranteed; and accordingly, the Government of every State shall, subject to section 8 of this Constitution, ensure their existence under a Law which provides for the establishment, structure, composition, finance and functions of such councils'. This provision, contrary to the unceasing caretaker committee system practiced in many states across the country, suggests that local council leaders are to be elected.

1. 9. Historical Development of Local Government

The development of local government system since its beginning in England went through four stages: the first was its early development; the second is the Mediaeval Period; the third is the Tudor Period and the fourth is the Eighteenth Century Local Government[13] which are described as below.

1.9.1. Early Development of Local Government

A study of local government cannot be complete without at least a cursory glance at the early beginning of this vital system for provision, operation and maintenance of essential public services at local level.

Richards' has described how the three traditional units of local government in England and Wales have been the county, the parish and the borough, each possessing a considerable degree of

---

13   Internet.

independence. Central interference with local institutions varied over time but these institutions were generally allowed to attend to local needs in the manner in which they believed best, largely because of the poor communications and restricted resources in earlier times. National grants were not available until the 1840s and hence the scale of local activities was restricted. This resulted in the establishment of new or ad hoc bodies to provide services which the traditional authorities were unable or unwilling to offer.

1.9.2. Mediaeval Period of Local Government

During the Middle Ages, England was predominantly an agricultural country with a widely scattered population. At that time England was divided into counties. Each county was administered by a county court made up of freemen of the shire and presided over by the sheriff appointed by the Crown. Hart and Garner have emphasized that these courts were more akin to governmental assemblies than judicial bodies. Each county was divided into hundreds, of which there were about 700 in all, each administered by a hundred courts. At a lower level came the vill or township without a court, which constituted a rudimentary police authority and the manor, which was concerned primarily with agricultural matters. Largely outside county jurisdiction were the boroughs; that were engaged in trade and commerce and possessed certain privileges, some being granted by royal charters. The boroughs enjoyed separate parliamentary representation from the counties.

The voting of money for church purposes was the function of parishioners meeting in the vestry, using church wardens as their officers. The parish was later to acquire non-ecclesiastical functions.

1.9.3. Tudor Period of Local Government

The mediaeval system of local government based upon the sheriff and the county, hundred and manor courts fell into disuse and, in the first instance, and most of the duties were undertaken by justices of the peace appointed by the Crown on their circuits around the country. The Kings justices prevented the growth of power of nobles who might have threatened the unity of the kingdom.

New social and economic problems accompanied the growth of industry in the sixteenth century. The enclosure of common fields resulted in many unemployed serfs who urgently needed relief, and the dissolution of the monasteries by Henry VIII abolished a valuable source of poor relief. Increased commerce produced the need for a better system of road maintenance.

To meet these needs local government was reorganized on the basis of parish with Justices of the peace undertaking a coordinating and controlling role. A considerable body of new legislation followed. By the Statute of Highways 1555, each parish was to appoint two surveyors responsible for the repair of roads in the parish, and the inhabitants required to devote four days' labour a year to the maintenance work. Wealthier persons could pay a highway rate in lieu of work, and this money was used to pay the working on the roads. The administrative duties of the parish were greatly increased by the Poor Relief Act 1601. Each parish had to appoint an overseer who recovered a rate from local inhabitants for the purchase of materials on which the poor could work. It seldom proved to be practicable to provide the work and it was largely replaced by the distribution of relief financed by a parish rate. Hence each parish carried out its duties through four categories of unpaid officer-overseer of the poor, surveyor, constable and church warden.

1.9.4. The Eighteenth Century Local Government

Central administrative control over Justices of the peace ceased after the Revolution of 1688. Quarter sessions operated as the principal link between central and local administration. This body consisted of all the county Justices of Peace and met at least four times a year. When dealing with administrative matters, Quarter sessions followed judicial procedure in the early part of the century. Later the approach changed when the Justices adjourned into a private meeting to discuss "county business", following the judicial work. The number of county officers increased, they attended the quarterly meetings and were largely responsible for the execution of the discussions.

1.10. Representative or Unrepresentative Local Government

Local government can be representative or it can be unrepresentative.

1.10.1. Representative Local Government

If a local government is self-governing, it means that local officials are elected by local people. There is a periodic election from time to time and these officials are responsible before the local election.

1.10.2. Unrepresentative Local Government

Officials who run local government may be held accountable before the people. For instance, head of a municipal council is a civil servant and institution is a local government unit.

1.11. Purpose of Local Government

The purpose of local government is to provide a system under which Councils perform the functions and exercise the powers conferred by or under the Local Government Act and any other Act for the peace, order and good government of municipal districts.

Local government serves a two-fold purpose:

1. The first purpose is the administrative purpose of supplying goods and services.

2. The second purpose is to represent and involve citizens in determining specific local public needs and how these local needs can be met.

Local representative government is a process that spans and connects representation and administration at local levels within local government structures. In order to understand the function and structure of local government, it is important to define local government and understand the meaning of local government democracy and values.[14]

The significance of local government will be addressed. With these aspects of local government in mind, attention will be directed towards the typical structure of local government as the administrative structure of local government forms the basic framework where in local public policy is determined and implemented. Therefore attention will be directed to the composition of councils and activities.

1.12. Multipurpose or Single Purpose of Local Government

Local Government can be a multipurpose body or single purpose body.

1.12.1. Multipurpose of Local Government

In multipurpose the local government has diversified responsibilities. It performs multiple tasks such as managing schools, health, and maintenance of roads, fire services and regulatory responsibilities.

---

14   "The Role and Purpose of Local Government," (upetd.up.ac.za/thesis/submitted/ etd-06222005-135528/…/03 chapter 3.pdf by B Havenga-2002).

1.12.2. Single Purpose Local Government

At the same time Local Government can also be a single purpose body. That means it can only have one function to perform. For example, usually in USA there is a single purpose bodies to avoid overlapping and chaos.

1.13. Duties and Responsibilities of Local Government

Local government remains a sphere of government with limited legislative power and authority that operates within clearly defined geographical and legal jurisdiction. The defining feature of local government is the authority to enact legislation within the defined jurisdiction.

Local government is comprised of a number of local authorities. Local authorities are created to render services in defined geographical areas, primarily because of the inability of central government to attend to all the detailed requirements of society that have to be satisfied by government institutions. The range of urban services provided by local authorities in developing countries, more particularly in Africa are, inter alia, parks, street cleaning, sanitation, refuse collection, road construction and maintenance, housing, water and sewerage, primary education, clinics, residential and industrial estates, planning and zoning, fire and ambulance services, camping sites and recreational services.

Local government is an essential link in the relationship between the government and the citizenry, especially because it is bound to particular geographical areas, and to the people who are affected by the problems that are peculiar to those areas. This enables local government to better understand and address these problems. Local governments are also instruments for greater community participation, because they have jurisdiction over fewer people than do higher levels of government. Consequently, they provide more channels and opportunities to utilize the talents, insights and creative abilities of individual citizens. These channels can also be referred to as the structure of local government which is comprised of various role players striving towards the common goal of delivering a service to the community. The council is the main organ within the structure of local government. A council is an essential part of every unit of local representative government.

Local government, then, is an essential instrument of national or state government which unites the people of a defined area in a common organization whose functions are essentially complementary to those of the central government and in the interests of the local residents since they satisfy common community needs. All communities have problems and needs which are shared by their citizens and which can be alleviated only by their joint actions, generally through government. Just as government in general is the means by which all the people can do jointly what they cannot do, or cannot do as economically or as effectively, acting alone, so local government is the means by which the residents of a local community can together accomplish what neither the national or state government not the individual residents can accomplish as adeptly alone.

The local government has its own duties that affect the daily lives of its residents. Local government offices provide services to residents, such as utility offerings and maintenance of public roads. The duties and responsibilities of local government are as hereunder:

1. **Elections**: Local governments are responsible for holding elections, both to elect local officials and as part of state and national elections. Local governments must provide convenient polling places, hire workers and ensure the security and fairness of the process. At the same time, local governments must oversee

their own elections and tabulate votes for positions such as mayor, county supervisor and other posts like sheriff's offices and school boards.

2. **Road Work**: Local governments are also charged with building and maintaining local roads. This includes street repair, expanding shoulders and painting clear lines for traffic to see and control traffic; making sure all intersections have appropriate safety signage; and providing adequate parking facilities. In addition to building and repairing roads, local governments must also provide snow removal and the salting and sanding of ice, drainage and sewer services and other services to keep the roads safe.

3. **Utilities**: One of the duties of local governments is to provide public utilities, like electricity, natural gas, and water and garbage collection. In some cases local governments perform these tasks directly, while other local governments contract with a private utility provider to supply service to residents.

4. **Public Safety**: Local governments are also responsible for the majority of public safety agencies and provisions. Those include institutions like fire departments, police departments and an ambulance service. In cases of emergency, federal and state personnel may be dispatched to help local public safety institutions. Local governments are responsible for staffing, as well as funding those groups, though higher levels of government typically contribute grants and other support. Also, local governments must determine and enforce safety codes, including building codes and other ordinances.

5. **Education:** Education constitutes one of the most important needs that the local governments must deal with. Local governments work in conjunction with state and federal government

to provide residents with access to public school system. On a local level, city councils must provide funding for the schools for transportation, hiring new teachers and finding a way to offer as much education as possible on a limited budget. Local governments work with state and federal governments to maintain a public school system. In some cases two or more local governments may share a single school system, especially in suburban and rural areas. The local government is responsible for hiring teachers, building school facilities and providing student transportation. State funding is an important part of local school district budgets, so adhering to state standards is another part of the local government's responsibility.

6. **Parks and Recreation**: Local government is responsible for maintaining access to recreation and parks departments that are safe for residents. The government is responsible for maintaining and staffing recreational facilities, like sports fields and parks, public buildings such as community halls and Scout halls. Any city parks, school parks or other public parks fall under the jurisdiction of local government. They must hire individuals to take care of all landscaping, cleanup, maintenance and any other responsibilities that come with maintaining a clean and safe public parks system, and providing residents with safe recreation opportunities. The nature of this task varies widely with region, size and affluence of a community. Local parks and recreation facilities range from flower gardens along highways to state-of-the-art gymnasiums, libraries and sports fields.

7. **Health and Human Services**: A local government's health and human services office provide residents with food stamps and Medicaid applications, shelter expense assistance, utility expense assistance and other forms of assistance to those in need.

8. **Funding**: The local government needs to maintain a funding base for different projects, including funding through taxes, funding through grants and other support. State funding is also essential for local school district budgets.

9. **Vital Records**: Local governments are typically the keepers of vital records such as deeds and marriage licenses. They also partner with state governments for motor vehicle and boat licensing.

1.14. Functions of Modern Government and Local Government

Modern government and local government, each has specific functions distinct from each other and are specified as below.

1.14.1. Functions of Modern Government

Major functions of modern government include:

1. Foreign diplomacy;
2. Military defense;
3. Maintenance of domestic order;
4. Administration of justice;
5. Protection of civil liberties;
6. Provision for and regulation of the conduct of periodic elections; and
7. Provision for public goods and services.

1.14.2. Functions of Local Government

Local government administration is usually broken up into three functional areas: political, civil service and judicial. A council or board of representatives is elected to serve and make local laws. This body has an elected leader or mayor. The civil service area is made up of employed staff or professionals to carry out the work of the local authority. The judicial area is made up of judges, justices and commissioners to serve in local courts. The functions of local government are as follows:

1. **Services:** Local administrations are responsible for delivering services to the population. These include: emergency services such as police, fire and paramedic services; public water and sewerage; planning; maintaining local environmental health; garbage collection; local highways maintenance and public transportation. Other provided services include recording births, deaths and marriages and legal transactions relating to properties and businesses. The administration manages public burial sites and cemeteries, public parks, open spaces and other public land within the jurisdiction.[15]

2. **Finance:** Local administrations have the power to raise money through property taxes on residences and businesses. They also receive revenue from fines, permits and other fees gathered from the population. Some jurisdictions have the power to levy additional sales taxes to support local services. Most jurisdictions receive additional funding and revenue from higher levels of government for services such as infrastructure, health, education, defense and environmental protection.

3. **Less Common Administrative Functions:** Some local government administrations control services typically supplied by the private sector. These services can include utilities management like electricity supply or production, water supply, gas distribution and telephone services. Separate administrative structures and corporations are set up with political oversight and nonprofit status.

4. **Economic Development:** Local administrations are required

---

to attract new businesses, private investment and people to their area through economic development. They play a role in attracting state-and federal-funded programmes that will derive a local economic benefit and create employment. Administrations also support tourism and visitor attraction programmes to bring additional revenue to local businesses.

1.15. Powers of Local Government and the State

Powers not granted to the federal government are reserved for states and the people, which are divided between state and local governments. Police departments, libraries, and schools, not to mention driver's licenses and parking tickets, usually fall under the oversight of state and local governments.

1.16. Role of Local Government in Rural Development

The federal and state governments offer public money for local economic development efforts. Economic and cultural realities differ even among towns in the same county. Local governments and agencies play a key role in managing funds.

One of the roles played by local government in rural development is the identification of the needs. A bureaucrat handling federal or state grant appropriations know the needs of tens of thousands of communities across the state. One rural community might need a highway work to attract business while another might need a new sewer system. Communities must identify their own needs and request funds from the appropriate agencies. The US Department of Agriculture operates offices in many counties to help local governments identify sources of federal funding.

The other role played by local government in rural development is administration of funds. Most federal and state economic development programmes allow local government applicants to administer expenditures, whether they include grants or loan programmes. Counties and local governments may handle the funds directly or allow a development organization to administer the programmes.

The third role played by local government in rural development is tax abatements. Economic development in rural areas depends directly on retaining and expanding existing companies and attracting new ones. Variations in local taxes can be the deciding factor for companies considering an expansion or relocation. Researchers at Ohio State University found that many local governments offer tax abatements designed to attract business to the area.[16]

1.17. Role of Local Government during a Crisis

The 9/11 terrorist attack on New York City and the devastation of New Orleans caused by hurricane Katrina highlight the importance of local government's role during a crisis. The role of local government is to ensure public safety and to respond with emergency management services, such as police, fire and medical care when a crisis strikes. Local government is usually the first to respond when a crisis unfolds, and is chiefly responsible for coordinating and deploying emergency management resources until the situation is brought under control and the public is safe. The roles played by local government during crisis are as follows;[17]

1. **Planning and Preparation**: Local governments plan and prepare for a crisis. Preparation usually involves developing an emergency preparedness plan outlining a series of actions for local government agencies to take when a disaster occurs. In certain cases, disaster preparations drills are performed to test

16   By Christie Gross, eHow Contributor.
17   Ibid

local government's ability to respond effectively. In addition, planning involves educating citizens about how to effectively deal with a crisis.

2. **Notification**: Local government puts a system in place for citizens to notify local government officials of a crisis. A 9/11 emergency dispatch services for citizens to report a crime or incident by phone is usually available for citizens to use. This type of system is used to initiate a response from first-responders as well as to coordinate the delivery of emergency management services…a function of local government.

3. **Communication**: Local government is responsible for communicating information about a crisis to the citizens. For example, local government officials must alert citizens of a disaster and provide them instructions which will enable them to protect themselves and their property when a crisis is imminent. Officials must also provide regular status updates when a disaster occurs, and then alert citizens when it's safe to resume normal activities. Officials generally rely on a mixed approach for alerting citizens of a disaster, including radio, TV and Internet communications, among others.

4. **Response**: Local government leads the coordination and management of first-responders during a crisis. In addition, local government officials are responsible for notifying state and federal law enforcement and emergency management services when additional aid is needed. It's the role of local government to administer aid when it's provided. Moreover, local government is also involved in resource coordination and distribution when nonprofit aid organizations are deployed to provide supplies and resources to displaced citizens. The response of local government generally involves multiple recovery phases,

especially those involving mass destruction of infrastructure and property as well as loss of lives.

5. **Review**: When crisis is over, local government officials review the circumstances around the crisis and efforts of personnel to end it. Information is conveyed to the public with help from the local media as an assessment of local government's ability to carry out its functions of public safety and emergency management. In essence, how well did the local government carry out its disaster preparation plan? The mayor is usually held accountable by citizens for his/her handling of the crisis.

1.18. Continuity or Discontinuity of Local Government

Local government can be of any type; either a continues organization or discontinues organization depending on the political structure of the country. When local government works in a continues manner then it continues but due to some political reasons it can be discontinued.

CHAPTER
TWO

LOCAL GOVERNMENT DEMOCRACY

2.1. Introduction

Local government is the third level of government deliberately created to bring government to the grass-roots population and gives the grass-roots population a sense of involvement in the political processes that control their daily lives. Democracy denotes a political system in which the eligible people participate actively not only in determining who governs them, but also in shaping the policy output of their government. The composition of government is usually determined in free and fair elections supervised by an impartial body. Gildenhuys *et al* (1991: 124) are of the opinion that there are specific democratic values that can serve as guiding principles for local government management and development. These democratic values will, therefore, be analyzed.

2.2. Local Government and Democratic Values

The reconciliation of conflict through local policy and decision making identifies common collective needs and the equitable allocation and application of scarce public resources amongst competing needs. As indicated in Gildenhuys *et al* (1991: 124), these values are as follows:

1. The application of resources must satisfy the collective needs of individuals. The object of local government is to serve individuals in communities. In democratic theory, local government exists for the sake of the individual and the individual does not exist to support the local government financially or otherwise.

2. Direct participation in decision making by citizens. This could be achieved through town meetings in small communities and through ratepayer associations, vigilante groups and social/political associations in larger communities. Direct or indirect public participation and decision making is an imperative for democratic local government.

3. Valuing responsibility and accountability arising from the tenets of democracy. Councilors must be sensitive to public problems and needs, feel responsible for satisfying those needs and problems and realize their accountability to the public. This calls for frequent interaction between councilors and the electorate.

4. Taking responsibility for management of programme effectiveness in order to ensure that needs are satisfied efficiently and effectively.

5. Social equity emanating from the tenets of democracy. The conventional and classical philosophy of local government and management revolves around the following:

   a. Municipal services rendered by local authorities should enhance social equity.

b. One of the main principles of social equity is the maintenance of high ethical and moral standards.

The effective implementation of democratic values requires
councilors and officials with integrity, which in turn demands
fairness, reasonableness and honesty. Social equity may also demand
that local government development should take place in such a
manner that the rule of law will prevail (Cloete, 1993: 24-25). In
the context of local government this means in accordance with
Gildenhuys et al (1991: 125), that:

i. Local authorities should not be allowed to exercise discretionary powers that are too wide and unrestrained and nor should
they be allowed to act in an arbitrary manner;
ii. All citizens should be equal under local law and should be
treated equally in terms of such law;
iii. the judiciary should function independently of local authorities
and judges; and
iv. Magistrates should act as independent guardians to ensure that
the rights and freedom of individuals is respected.

Social equity requires the support of well known tenets of
democracy. The objective of democracy is to create conditions
under which each individual may achieve his greatest welfare and
prosperity (Cloete, 1993: 25). The machinery of local government
should be organized in such a way that it will allow mutual deliberation and consultation to attain the objectives of democracy.
Caution should be exercised at all times to ensure that the interests
of one group are not unfairly prejudiced or those of another unjustly
favoured. Furthermore, there should be no secrecy in local government administration. The citizenry observing or investigating the

particular activity should have the right and freedom to express their views on the matter. With democratic values in mind, it is important to focus on the significance of local government.

2.3. The Significance of Local Government

The existence of local government has always been defended on the basis that local government is a crucial aspect of the process of democratization and intensification of mass participation in the decision making process. It is furthermore argued that no political system is considered to be complete and democratic if it doesn't have a system of local government (Mawhood, 1993: 66; cf. also Wraith, 1964: 118).

A number of reasons have been advanced as to why a system of local government is essential. These reasons are:
1. Training ground for mass political education;
2. training ground for political leadership; and
3. That it facilitates government accountability.

The aforementioned forms a crucial part of the need for the existence of local government. The role and purpose of local government is furthermore strengthened when these reasons for it are considered.

2.3.1. Local Government as a Training Ground for Mass Political Education

The system of local government has been advocated and supported as it is generally believed that the system of local government serves as a training ground and nursery for mass political education and mobilization in this regard. Tocqueville (1935: 631) remarks as follows:

"Town meetings are to liberty what primary schools are to science: they bring it within the people's reach, they teach men how to use and how to enjoy."

While, Marshall (1965: 59) is more explicit stating the following:

"A principal objective of local government is that it should foster the specious demagogue, to avoid electing the incompetent or corrupt representative, to debate issues effectively, to relate expenditure to income, to think for tomorrow."

This does not imply that the mere existence of local government will automatically lead to the development, nourishment and maturation of a public spirit of political awareness and consciousness. Intensive political mobilization programmes must be introduced by these institutions to galvanize the public into active and meaningful political involvement. This will enable people to see the usefulness of local government and their role in the process of decision making. Conscious political work by local government councilors, carried out with the explicit and vowed aim of intensifying, accelerating and directing the participation of people in local politics lets the public sees local government as just another bureaucratic government institution (Holm, 1971: 61).

2.3.2. Local Government as a Training Ground for Political Leadership

Local government is essential as it provides training ground for political leadership, especially for those intending to venture into the arena of national politics, and in this regard Laski (1931: 31) remarks:

"If members (MPs) were, before their candidature was legal, required to serve three years on a local body, they would gain the feel of institutions so necessary to success."

There is some merit in this logic, but it cannot be logically deduced that legislators with some experience in local government politics are better national legislators than those without it. There is no doubt that participation in local government politics provide an opportunity for councilors to gain experience in the mechanics of politics such as the process of law-making and budgeting (Laski, 1931: 31). Letting councilors experience the mechanics of politics has impact on the restructuring of local government.

2.3.3. Local Government as a Facilitation of Government Accountability

Local government is generally seen as a defense mechanism against arbitrary power of government as it is a means whereby an unhealthy concentration of power at the centre is prevented. Local government, as it is claimed, discourages the tyranny of the centralization of power and, in this regard Smith (1985: 27) states that:

"There is some truth in the proposition that local democracy provides for greater accountability and control than field administration, public corporate and appointed agencies. The processes involved in local government make accountability more meaningful because of the elective elements linking bureaucrat and citizen. The political activities inherent in local government, i.e. elections, rule-making, political pressure, publicity and public debate-close the gap between the citizen and the administration and provide opportunities for grievances to be aired and wrong remedied."

Whilst the above may be true, there is a strong feeling that local government is, unfortunately, prone to corruption (Olowu, 1988: 12). Furthermore, Stewart (1983: 8) remarks in this regard:

"Where such accusations are made, and justifiably so, they are made because of the very visibility of local governments. There is no official secret act guarding even routine decisions from public scrutiny. Committees of local authorities generally meet in public and their agendas are open in ways that would horrify civil servants or central politicians. The system is open and provides thereby correctives to reveal defects."

Commenting on the African situation with regard to complaints that local governments are prone to corruption, Olowu (1988:20) observes that:

"When the first books of corruption in African countries were published, they concentrated on local government level. Local governments in some parts of Africa were described as a conspiracy against the public, an institution that is riddled with 'bribery, nepotism, politics and corruption.' Over the years, as more documentation on corruption in central governments has accumulated, it has become evident that corruption is a universal problem for all governments in all countries."

The argument is persuasive and has merit, for the central government is not only geographically distant but also psychologically and socially distant. In developing countries a physical infrastructure is necessary to facilitate communication between the central government and the people. A local government can therefore become a viable and flexible instrument for promoting and facilitating good governance and public accountability. Meanwhile, Held (1987: 15) aptly comments in this regard that:

"The affairs of government and national politics are not things many claim to understand, nor are they a source of sustained interest. Significantly, those closest to the centres of power and privilege are the ones who indicate the most interest in and are most favourable to political life. However, it may well be that those who express lack of interest in politics do so precisely because they experience 'politics' as remote, because they feel it does not directly touch their lives and/or that they are powerless to affect its course."

Local government may, therefore, assist to put some measure of power in the hands of the masses, thereby making the notion of government of people, by the people, and for the people a little more realistic. Latib (1995: 8) in this regard, remarks:

"Far too much attention has historically been placed on compliance and process ... what is needed is the building of a broader community perception of accountability ... This broader perspective implies that accountability should be based on an overall concept of governance. This approach emphasizes not only political representation and the supremacy of political structures in the accountability process, but also interactive processes with civil society."

Conceptualized in this way, accountability becomes an integral component of the democratic process. Local government can go a long way to enriching accountability. Accountability may require extensive efforts to remove or at least reduce the cynicism of the 'ordinary' people, and the absolutely poor who see politics as a sophisticated game designed by a small clique of power holders to manipulate and cheat them (Holm, 1989). For the 'ordinary' people and the absolutely poor have come to believe that government by the majority is merely a tantalizing mask, an illusion, which masks what really happens in the body politic. The body politic is embodied in the structure of local government.

2.4. The Structure of Local Government

The administrative structure of local government is the framework within which local public policy is determined and implemented. The structure of an organization not only determines the relationship between the organs but also its character and strength.

A distinction must be drawn between formal static structures and the more informal kinetic structures. The static structures may be reduced to a set of laws and an organizational chart, which diagrams the skeleton and organs. The informal structures, by contrast, form complex living bodies, which are best described in terms of what the body does rather than how it is made up. The Council and its committees as legislative authorities and, the Chief Executive Officer and staff as administrative authorities will therefore be discussed as the organs of deliberation and representation.

2.4.1. The Council

The council is the main representative organ of local government. A council is an essential part of every unit of local representative government. The role of the council as a representative body varies with the evolution and the mechanics of the processes of local government in each country. The degree to which a local unit has a representative government depends largely on two factors.

One factor is the extent to which the membership of a council represents and is answerable to the public, and the other factor is the extent to which the council has the authority and power to define local policy objectives and to have these objectives implemented (Humes & Martin, 1969: 80-81).

A unit of local representative government has one or more representative organs with some authority to govern. Almost invariably one of these organs is the council, which offers the opportunity to discuss and give advice on local issues, but also has the responsibility for making decisions authorizing or directing the local staff to perform tasks. The council makes decisions by such acts as passing the budget, enacting ordinances and by-laws and making or approving appointments (Humes & Martin, 1969: 82). The council approves and in many cases amends proposals submitted to it, and generally may take the initiative in making proposals. A council with decisive authority may take decisions regarding matters of overall policy objectives or of relatively more minor matters concerning the routine coordination of staff (Humes & Martin, 1969: 82).

The number of members of local councils varies, in general, with the population of the unit of local government. The size of councils, however, is also closely interrelated to their role in local government structures. The largeness or the smallness of the council affects its representative character, its effectiveness and the nature of its deliberations (Humes & Martin, 1969: 86).

Large councils must rely heavily on the executive organs, or on the committees of council or both, to be effective. A large council makes it possible to have more citizens participate in local government work, therefore making local government more representative and closer to the people. Size is a relatively minor factor in the determination of the representative character of a council; more important are the methods of selection and the degree to which the members of council can responsibly and effectively represent the will of the electorate. A council with a very small membership often allows little opportunity for the expression of minority opinions and may thus be at a disadvantage in knowing the thinking, desires and needs of the people (Humes & Martin, 1969: 86-88).

Private citizens appointed to the council are selected for a variety of reasons. Upon appointment to the council these private citizens are referred to as councillors. Councillors may be leading citizens who contribute wisdom to the discussions of council and stature to its public image. Councillors may also be political supporters of the party leadership, which controls the nomination, or they may represent minority groups whom it is politically advantageous to include on the council. Appointed councillors are frequently among the hardest workers in council activities (Laski, 1936: 87). Supporters of the appointment method of selecting councillors emphasize the importance of having some members who can afford to ignore the political pressures faced by those who must contest elections. Appointed members are more sensitive to the wishes of the political leadership responsible for their appointment than to public sentiment. Terms of office of a councillor, therefore, should be short enough to provide for electoral control, but long enough to provide time effective action and continuity (Steiner, 1956: 190).

2.4.1.1. Duties, Roles and Responsibilities of a Councilor

A councilor is the representative of a local area. A councilor's primary role is to represent his/her ward or division and the people who live in it. Councilors provide a bridge between the community and the council.

The elected council is the policy-making arm of the local authority, the members of which act by what are termed 'reserved functions' which are defined by law and specified across a whole range of enactments. These comprise mainly decisions on important matters of policy and finance, such as, adoption of annual budget, development plan, bye-laws.

Because of the role local authorities' play, the range of matters for which they are responsible and their closeness to local communities, local government has a more immediate effect on the day-to-day lives of the people than most other sectors of public administration.

A council is the only other institution whose members are directly elected by all of the people. Local government has, therefore, both a representational and an operational role, with responsibility for a range of services.

Councils' roles are as set out below:

1. Act as representative, informed and responsible decision makers in the interests of their communities;
2. Provide and coordinate various public services and facilities and to develop their communities and resources in a socially just and ecologically sustainable manner;
3. Encourage and develop initiatives within their communities for improving the quality of life within them;
4. Represent the interests of their communities to the wider community; and
5. Exercise, perform and discharge the powers, functions and duties of Local Government in relation to their areas, as contained in the Local Government Act, and other Acts.

2.4.1.2. Functions of the Councils

Councils' functions are as hereunder:

1. Plan at the local and regional level for the development and future requirements of their areas;
2. Provide services and facilities that benefit their areas, ratepayers and residents, and to visitors to their areas;
3. Provide for the welfare, well being and interests of individuals and groups within their communities;
4. Take measures to protect their areas from natural and other hazards and to mitigate the effects of such hazards;
5. Manage, develop, protect, restore, enhance and conserve the environment in an ecologically sustainable manner, and to improve amenity;
6. Provide infrastructure for their communities and for development within their areas;
7. Promote their areas and to provide an attractive climate and locations for the development of business, commerce, industry and tourism;
8. Establish or support organizations or programs that benefit people in their areas or Local Government generally;
9. Manage and, if appropriate, develop public areas vested in or occupied by a Council;
10. Manage, improve and develop resources available to a council; and
11. Undertake other functions and activities conferred by or under an Act.

2.4.1.3. Objectives of the Councils

Councils' objectives are set out as below:
1. To provide open, responsive and accountable government;
2. To be responsive to the needs, interests and aspirations of individuals and groups within their communities;

3. Participating with other councils, and with State and national governments, in setting public policy and achieving regional, State and national objectives;

4. Giving due weight–in all their plans, policies and activities–to regional, State and national objectives and strategies concerning the economic, social, physical and environmental development and management of the community;

5. Seeking to co-ordinate with State and national governments in the planning and delivery of services in which those governments have an interest;

6. Seeking to ensure a proper balance within their communities between economic, social, environmental and cultural considerations;

7. Managing their operations and affairs in a manner that emphasizes the importance of service to the community;

8. Seeking to ensure that council resources are used fairly, effectively and efficiently; and

9. Seeking to provide services, facilities and programs that are adequate and appropriate and ensuring equitable access to its services, facilities and programs wherever possible.

2.4.1.4. Focus on the Roles, Functions and Objectives of the Councils

Councils' roles, functions and objectives focus on the following:

1. Representing everyone in the community, preparing strategic management plans and making decisions about priorities for services and facilities in the council area.

2. Encouraging participation with other councils, regions and State and Commonwealth Governments in setting public policy and in the planning and delivery of services.

3. Providing equity in access to services for the wellbeing of people who live and work in their communities, and striking a balance between social, environmental and economic priorities.
4. Representing the interests of the local community to the wider community, including to State and Commonwealth Governments about what needs to be done locally.
5. Providing open, responsive and accountable Government, and ensuring the available resources are used fairly, efficiently and effectively.

2.4.1.5. The Council Chairperson and the Secretary

No council can operate without a chairperson. The function of the chairperson is to promote and maintain orderly discussion within the council. The chairperson is responsible for order and his/her unique position of being the focus of all remarks in the course of a council meeting provides him/her with ample opportunities for guiding the discussions (Wheare, 1955: 39-40).

The chairperson has some opportunity to influence council decisions by virtue of his/her participation in the developing of the agenda for the council session. Usually this is drawn up in cooperation with the secretary or clerk. The chairperson is a crucial position to determine what items will be discussed and in what order. The chairperson moderates or controls the discussion (Wheare, 1955: 39-40). The chairperson exerts influence over the discussion and decisions by recognizing and encouraging speakers as well as by discouraging others, by the manner in which he accepts, defers and declines motions and amendments and even by timing of calls for meetings. The chairperson is expected to exercise an impartial role. Council election is the general method for choosing a chairperson (Humes & martin, 1969: 96).

A secretary of council has the task of recording the minutes, keeping the records and usually the actual preparing of the agenda. This official must work closely with the council chairperson and usually is in a strategic position to give the latter advice on the initiation and guidance of council deliberations. Usually the council secretary is a salaried full-time career official in the local administration. His/her knowledge of administration and his/her experience in local government make his/her advice valuable and therefore less likely to be ignored (Humes & Martin, 1969: 96-97).

2.4.1.6. The Executive Committee

Due to the limited size of the council it is difficult for the council as single structure to perform all the actions necessary within local government. Therefore certain supportive structures have been created to assist the council in the execution of its tasks. One of these structures is the Executive Committee. The Executive Committee is an executive organ of a unit of local government that has the central overall task of directing, initiating and coordinating all or most of the activities of the unit. There are three essential, interdependent duties of an executive organ: initiation, integration and interpretation. An executive organ is expected to take the initiative in developing and implementing those measures, which are in the best interests of the public and those that are necessary for the efficient administration of local services. A second essential duty of an executive organ is integration; it is expected to integrate and coordinate all the various local activities into one effective whole. Another essential duty of an executive organ is interpretation for the making and implementing of policy is one continuous process of exposition. Policy objectives must be interpreted to those who help with implementation if the tasks are to be carried out meaningfully (Humes & Martin, 1969: 113-114).

The executive committee of a local government is a plural executive organ composed of elected persons. It is responsible to the council and generally has fewer than eight members. The elected persons on the executive committee are chosen by and from the council. The term of office of the elected executive committee members coincides with the term for the council (Urwick, 1957: 44-45).

The tasks of the executive committee could be divided according to two different points of view. The one viewpoint is from the side of the council to whom the executive committee is responsible; the other viewpoint is from the side of the staff for whose activities the executive committee is responsible. In the representative aspects of the process of local government, the executive committee is the steering committee of the council and is expected, along with the chief executive officer, to provide overall initiative in the policy making process. The executive committee also goes over the council agenda and makes recommendations on the items to be discussed and the final form of the proposals to be submitted to the council. An executive committee generally has broad latitude to exercise discretion as long as decisions are in accord with policy as determined by the council. The executive committee usually also has a fairly broad power to make decisions on matters which come up between council sessions and cannot be held over until a succeeding meeting. The executive committee is responsible for the overall coordinated implementation of the decisions of the council (Locke, 1957: 1-7).

The importance of the executive committee is demonstrated by the fact that the chairperson is almost invariably the most important single position in the local government structure from which the formulation, exposition and implementation of municipal policy can be influenced. The role of the executive committee chairperson is dependent on the extent of his executive power, both within the executive committee and in other capacities. It is inevitable that the collective power of the executive committee is focused to some extent on the chairperson. The prerogatives of the chairperson as presiding officer of the executive committee meetings provide him/her with a natural opportunity to present ideas, guide discussions and influence decisions (Locke, 1957: 1-7). The capacity of the chairperson to focus this collective power in him/her is strengthened by the fact that he/she is usually accepted by most, if not all, of the executive committee members, as well as the council, as the leader and representative of the executive committee.

The executive committee considers matter referred to it by the standing committees and special committees. An analysis of the functions and composition of these committees follows hereunder.

2.4.1.7. Special and Standing Committees of the Council

A distinction has to be made between standing committees and special committees. Special committees, or ad hoc committees, are appointed for a special task and their existence is expected to terminate upon completion of that task. A standing committee is a continuing body although its membership may change. A standing committee is considered to be permanent, at least until there is a general reorganization of the system of committees of a council. Standing committees play more important roles in the continuing process of local government (Laski, 1936: 82).

Most committees specialize in matters dealing with one particular geographical area, activity or management aspect of local government. The majority of council committees are set up to deal with matters affecting a particular purpose or activity, such as libraries, education or public health. Often the arrangement of these committees corresponds to a certain degree with the organization of the departments of the local authority. This arrangement along so-called vertical lines allows the education standing committee, for instance, to work closely with the education department. The decisions of the committees must receive the approval of the council (Wheare, 1955: 66). A council, through its leaders, may exercise its control over committee decisions that may be exercised through informal contacts between committee and council leaders.

The size of the committee can vary considerably, but generally the size ranges between three and twenty members. An argument for the use of committees is that it enables fewer people than the whole council to be associated with a particular process. The workload of the council is passed on to smaller organs, which may more thoroughly assess relevant factors in making a decision. When the committees themselves are too large to deal with the volume of work presented to them, the committees tend to subdivide into smaller bodies or working groups. A committee may be used though, not just to enable fewer people to be associated with a particular process but also to enable more people to be associated with a particular process (Humes & Martin, 1969: 100-102). The smaller membership of a committee of council does not preclude the possibility of using committees as an opportunity to expand public participation in the representative governmental process.

The nominations of committee members are approved by councils. Councils form a small group of committees which consist mainly of council members. Generally a list of small groups of the members who should serve on which committees is prepared.

This small group is in some cases formally constituted as a special committee and usually consists of the most important individuals on the council with the council chairperson and majority party leadership usually having a key role in its deliberations. Usually a council member who has been selected to serve on a given committee continues in this position as long as he is re-elected to the council. The general practice is to include members from all parties represented on the council; however, committees are often packed with members of the majority party-either as a matter of patronage or to control decisions, or both (Robson, 1954: 39).

The committee chairperson and the secretary have positions of considerable importance. The chairperson is generally a senior or leading member of the committee who is selected by the committee itself or by the council. Once selected, a chairperson often continues to be re-elected to this post. To a large degree the effectiveness of the committee is dependent upon the chairperson's personality and ability, for the chairperson of a committee, like the chairperson of a council, can do much to determine the scope of discussions and guide the conclusions of the group over which he presides. In some cases a committee chairperson may exercise more power in his relations with his committee than a council chairperson can with regard to the council as a whole (Humes & Martin, 1969: 102-103).

A committee secretary, in some cases the chief administrative officer or his/her assistants and, in many cases, a department head, renders advice, furnishes statistical information and explains and answers criticism concerning the working of the department. He/she has to undertake the execution of any work after obtaining the financial and administrative sanction of the committee.

The council and its committees form the political or legislative authority. To implement the decisions of the political or legislative authority, an administrative authority is required. The administrative authority is comprised of the Executive Chief Officer, departmental heads and staff members.

2.4.1.8. Responsibilities of the Mayor

In every city or municipality the mayor is the responsible person for administration of the area. The mayor's responsibilities are primarily to preside at council meetings and to act as head of the city for ceremonial purposes and for purposes of military law. The mayor votes as a council member and does not have any veto power.

2.4.1.9. Duties and Roles of the Mayor

The Mayor exercises legal duties. The Mayor enforces all laws of the City. He/she signs all commissions, licenses, and permits granted by legislative authority, as well as other instruments that require his/her signature under the law. The Mayor serves as the top conservator of peace in the City.

The mayor in the city is responsible for hiring and firing staff, may have veto power and is responsible for implementing legislation passed by the council. The mayor is responsible for ceremonial duties, and some cities may give the mayor legislative power as well.

2.4.1.10. The Chief Executive Officer

In the past, the term Town clerk was used to refer to the position of Chief Executive Officer. This created confusion as this person was seen as the clerk of the council.

The post of the chief executive officer is essentially and

pre-eminently the focal point of a local government structure. He/she is the principal person coordinating the representative and staff aspects of the process of local government. As the focal point in the local government process, the chief executive officer works closely with the council in the development of policy and directs staff in implementing policies (Humes & Martin, 1969: 125-126). In many instances, he/she also aids the executive committee in coordinating these two aspects of government at a local level.

The day-to-day management of the local authority, including staffing matters, is vested in a full time chief executive. The chief executive and/or staff to whom functions are delegated discharge what are termed 'executive functions'—in effect these involve the day-to-day running of the authority within the policy parameters as determined by the council. Any function of a local authority that is not specified in law as a reserved function is deemed to be an executive function. The legal character of a local authority thus comprises two elements, the elected council of the authority and the chief executive, with responsibility for performing local author-ity functions shared between them. However, legally all functions, whether performed by the elected council or by the chief execu-tive, are exercised on behalf of the local authority.

The chief executive officer does not only take the leading part in formulating ideas, but also has an important role as the mobiliz-er of support for proposals. As the focus for the development of the proposals, he/she is expected by the council and the public to ensure their favourable consideration. The effective chief executive officer, either directly or indirectly, must not only build up enough support in the council so that his/her proposals are adopted but he/she and those council members who support his/her propos-als are re-elected to office (Ridley, 1959: 13). As the focal person charged with the coordination of the implementation of policy, he/she has the resources to find out about and thereafter explain the various technical aspects involved in carrying out decisions as well as how specific decisions will fit into overall local government policy (Humes & Martin, 1969: 127).

A decision of a representative organ remains practically meaningless until it is transformed into action. This indicates why the role of the chief executive officer as the head of the local staff is as important as his/her part in the formulation and exposition of decisions of the council and the executive committee. Invariably the use of executive power involves some exercise of discretion. The amount of discretion exerted depends partially on national and local customs, partially on the laws pertaining to the local unit, and partially on the rapport existing between the local chief executive and the other governmental organs, including the organs of higher units as well as local representative organs and staff (Steiner, 1956: 190). The local chief executive officer, as the apex of the administrative hierarchical pyramid, is charged with carrying out the overall policies made for the local unit by the organs of higher units of government or by local representative organs. He/she, often with the executive committee, therefore has the right and the duty to make such decisions as may be necessary to supplement and carry out the policies of higher units, or of local representative organs, or of both (Robson, 1954: 39). An essential aspect of this job is the duty to lead in preparing and controlling the execution of the budget. He/she has the duty to supervise the employees of local units, to coordinate their activities and to maintain their efficiency.

2.4.1.11. Roles of the Chief Executive

The day-to-day management of the local authority, including

staffing matters, is vested in a full time chief executive. The chief executive and/or staff to whom functions are delegated discharge what are termed 'executive functions' – in effect these involve the day-to-day running of the authority within the policy parameters as determined by the council. Any function of a local authority that is not specified in law as a reserved function is deemed to be an executive function.

2.5. The Staffs of Local Government

The staffs of a local government are the employees engaged in the preparation and implementation of local policies. Local governments with more than a few employees divide their staffs into departments, which constitute the major parts of the local staffs' structure. The primary consideration in the establishment of most departments is that they handle all matters affecting a particular purpose or activity or two or more closely related purposes or activities. For instance, a city might have a security department to deal with all matters affecting public security and a fire department dealing with all police and fire matters. Other departments may be organized to handle such activities as public works, water supply, education and health. Such departments are also known as line departments (Jackson, 1959: 104).

Other departments are organized to deal with matters affecting one or more aspects of the management of local government activities. There may be, for instance, a finance department, a legal department, a record department, personnel, or a building and supply department. These non-line departments' deal with matters that affect all local activities and thus every one of the departments, sometimes these are called auxiliary or staffs departments (Bromage, 1957: 324). Whereas the line departments exist primarily to serve the public and a large proportion of their employees work outside of their headquarters. The non-line departments exist primarily to assist the other departments in carrying out their activities. The non-line departments affect matters pertaining to all the departments, especially finance, and are therefore in a strategic position to coordinate and sometimes to control the activities of local units.

2.5.1. The Departmental Heads

Among the most important positions on the staff are the heads of departments. Not only do department heads direct the work of the employees in their respective departments, they also play an important part in the preparation and in the actual making of the decisions which determine the policies affecting their departments (Humes and Martin, 1969: 155-156).

The department heads work in close conjunction with the representative organs not only in carrying out the decisions of the councils, the executive committee and the standing committees, but also in preparing the papers which lay the groundwork for the decisions made by these bodies. The department heads report directly to the chief executive officer (Humes & Martin 1959: 155-157).

Departmental heads have responsibility for specific discipline within a local authority. For example, the departmental head of finance will take responsibility for the administration of finances and the implementation of financial policy within the local authority as derived from council resolutions. The departmental head of electricity will have the main responsibility for ensuring service delivery with regard to electricity function.

2.6. Concerns in Restructuring Local Government

Effective and optimal local government restructuring must be approached in a multi-disciplinary way involving the generic administrative processes and the environment. Application and adherence to the following principles in a multi-disciplinary fashion should substantially enhance the effectiveness and efficiency of local government.

a. Principles of good government;
b. Principles of megapolitics;
c. Constitutional and other legal principles;
d. The realities of the urban environment;
e. The impacts of the socio-political dimension; and
f. The principles of balanced application of all criteria.

The restructuring of local government should be done with the future in mind. Population growth, urbanization, the incidence of crime, economic development, technical developments and world-wide trends of privatization and decentralization of power should be recognized and incorporated in local government restructuring.

In addition, increasing international awareness of the environment makes it imperative that metropolitan areas are not separated from their rural linkages. Environmental management, including solid waste management and environmental protection, dictates that metropolitan areas should have some measure of control over adjacent rural areas.

2.7. Principle of Megapolitics and Increasing Globalization

African countries are part of the world and hence they function in an open system. Megatrends or megapolitics (Davidson & Rees-Mogg, 1992: 340) thus also have an impact on the African communities. Davidson and Rees-Mogg (1992: 35) identify four major megapolitical factors, i.e. topography, climate, technology and microbes. The latter three are already affecting African countries, for example, South Africa's position in relation to the world.

The climate severely affects African countries' long-term ability to be self-sufficient with regard to food and water and could place a limit on population growth and development. The use of computers in the industrialization process has widened the gap between high technology and emerging countries, making the emerging countries less competitive and more subservient to high technology nations. More importantly however, the use of technology has made the cost of power (i.e. weapons) affordable, and hence has shifted the power base from a historically centralized system to a decentralized system. Africa is also currently under severe threat from microbes, including AIDS, hepatitis, malaria and tuberculosis; and recently corona virus infectious disease (COVID-19 Pandemic).

Globalization, however much it is written about and debated, should never be underestimated and nor should the impact it has had on the African countries situation. The world has indeed shrunk to a village in which African countries' every move, for example in the political and economic fields, is clearly visible and immediately becomes part of the global debate.

The impact of globalization has also been recognized, for example, in South Africa, in Section 2.6 of the White Paper on Local Government March 1998, issued by the Department of Provincial Affairs and Constitutional Development.

No municipality can ignore the economic changes taking place in its locality, in the surrounding region, in the nation, and globally. The rise or decline of industries can have a marked impact on local income, employment and tax revenue.

Globalization, or the internationalization of capital, production, services and culture, has had, and will continue to have a major impact, in particular on metropolitan areas. The logic of transitional corporations, the fact that economic transactions and the integration of systems of production occur on a world-wide basis, and the rapid development of information technologies, have resulted in the emergence of the so-called 'global economy.' In this context large cities become the nodes or points of contact which connect economies across the globe.

The Growth, Employment and Redistribution (GEAR) strategy places greater emphasis on an export-oriented economy, and will lead to increased international openness and competition. The ultimate aim is to achieve internationally competitive industries and enhance economic growth and well-being. In the immediate term, municipalities will need to manage the consequences of globalization-such as the restructuring and relocation of industries.

Local government has an interest in attracting investment based on promoting the comparative advantages of the area for competitive industries as well as supporting the growth of local enterprises. It will become increasingly important for municipalities to find the right balance between competition and cooperation among themselves. While some competition will improve both efficiency and innovation, cooperation between South African municipalities is necessary to enhance the performance of the national economy as a whole, and to avoid damaging forms of competition between municipalities.

2.7.1. Legal Principles

The Constitution of a country and other laws determine the legal framework and nature of local government structures. The analysis of the legal environment is important in assessing the viability of a metropolitan area and in determining various restructuring options. An overview and assessment of the legal environment in conjunction with other relevant factors will enable decision-makers to take informed strategic decisions regarding the future of the metropolitans.

The Constitution, national legislation, state or provincial legislation as well as by-laws guide the operations of local government and provide the framework for determining restructuring options. It is therefore important that these sources of authority be viewed holistically in assessing issues of demarcation. Any demarcation design should derive its authority from the sources of legality and competence.

The ideas and visions of the lawmakers are manifested in laws which do create a total vision of what future local government should look like and provide a framework for determining municipal areas and guidelines for administrative systems as well as procedures for administering local government issues. Laws are not prescriptive about determining municipal viability or exact administrative and governance systems. Legislation does not prescribe which administrative system is the best for a specified municipal area, but only provides a framework and therefore local government officials; politicians and other stakeholders should determine the correct and optimal design for a municipal system.

Restructuring assessment and the development options are in essence a determination of the municipal system value chain. Laws provide a framework against which the system can be evaluated whilst true value realization is acquired through the application of strategy, structure and technology driven by a clear vision of a healthy metropolitan area.

2.7.2. The Urban Environment

Urban geographers use different ways to delimit urban populations, but often include the following criteria (Carter 1989: 6):

1. Size and population;
2. Density of population and housing;
3. Predominant type of economic activity;
4. Urban characteristics; and
5. Administrative function or structure.

In addition, several systems of classification have been designed to classify towns and urban areas. Jones (1990: 21), however, concludes that, at best, these models are still crude, as the models ignore common sense criteria and suggest that the concept of region is trying to capture a relationship that is becoming outdated.

A metropolitan area in its strictest sense refers to a mother city, for example, Cape Town in South Africa, with its dependent substructures for instance, Bellvile and Parow. The Gauteng Province in South Africa may be described as a conurbation, which initially was comprised of separate independent entities, but gradually grew into a massive integrated urban system (Van der Merwe, 1991: 53). The term metropolitan, however, is used widely in a loose format. For example, the World Bank (1993: 7) describes South Africa as follows:

"Nowhere is this concentration of people and economic activity more visible than in the four metropolitan areas-the PWV complex, Cape Town, Durban and Port Elizabeth … For South Africa, the reality of such demographic and economic concentrations is clear; without functioning cities, the ability to sustain overall economic recovery will be jeopardized. Designing a comprehensive urban strategy is therefore an important national priority for South Africa."

Meanwhile, Jones (1990: 53) describes the vision of the future metropolis as follows:

"The city of the future is already recognizable. It will be a city of suburbs, each more or less self-contained with its basic retail and public services, each with basically sound housing. There will be plenty of local, suburban jobs: an efficient highway system will provide good access to a wider variety of jobs across the city as a whole and to those services and social and recreational opportunities which cannot be obtained locally … What can be wrong with it?"

The restructuring of local government is not enough to ensure viable and sustainable urban areas. Managing the process of urbanization has become, and in the future will continue to be the critical factor for determining success.

2.7.3. The Socio-Political Dimension

Politicians and bureaucrats should be aware of the real needs and wants of the people. Berger (1988: 16) assumes that political interests for the middle classes are the same regardless of race. Political interests include:

1. Preserving of orderly suburban life;
2. Combating crime;
3. Preserving income and avoiding higher taxation;
4. Growing an efficient economy;
5. Fostering dependable civil service;
6. Having a social service that works; and
7. Ensuring a physically secure living and working environment.

2.7.4. A Socio-Political System Analysis

In the complex and interwoven field of local government and municipal systems management where there is a real or perceived effort to satisfy the needs and wants of people, there exists an increasing need to describe, evaluate and explain concepts of the urban system. To this extent the widely accepted model for socio-political systems analysis of David Easton can be applied as follows (Easton, 1965: 83):

1. Minimal Concepts for a Systems Analysis: A systems analysis provides for a more inclusive, more flexible and more expansive theoretical structure than is available in other comparative approaches. According to Easton (1965: 84), a system is defined as "… any set of variables regardless of the degree of interrelationship among them." This definition is also useful in describing urban systems as it frees us from the need to argue about whether an urban system is really a system. The only question of importance about a set of variables is whether this set constitutes useful one-does it helps us to understand and explain some aspects of human behaviour of concern to us? Does it do so in the case of the system in question, in this case an urban system?

To be of maximum use in describing urban systems, a socio-political system can be designated as "those interactions through which values are authoritatively allocated for a society" (Easton, 1965: 84). This would then also hold true for an element of urban systems such as demarcation because untimely demarcation has to do with the allocation of societal values in the form of boundaries. The environment within which the system dynamically exists may be divided into two parts, the intra-societal and the extra-societal.

The intra-societal aspect consists of those systems that form part of society but are excluded from the system itself by the definition of the nature of interactions. Intra-societal systems would include such sets of behaviour, attitudes and ideas as might be called the economy, culture, social structure or personalities. They are functional segments of the society with respect to which the system (urban system) itself is a component. In a given society the systems other than the urban system constitute a source of many influences that create and shape the conditions under which the urban system itself must operate.

The second part of environment-the extra societal-includes all those systems that lie outside the given society itself. They are functional components of an international society or what we might describe as the supra-society, a supra-system of which any single society is part.

Together these two classes of systems (the intra-and extra societal) may be described as the total environment of a system or the urban system. From these environmental sources arise influences that are of consequence for possible stresses on the urban system.

Disturbance is a concept that may be used to identify those influences from the total environment of the system that act upon it so that it is different after the stimulus from what it was before. Disturbances may be favourable with respect to the persistence of the system; others may be entirely neutral with respect to possible stress. Many disturbances can be expected to lead in the direction of system stress. As far as the model of Easton is concerned, the concept of system stress is fairly important. An urban system is recognized as being a system by virtue of the fact that it contributes to the successful fulfillment of two functions. An urban system must be able to allocate values for the society it serves and it must manage to induce most members to accept these allocations as binding, at least for most of the time.

South African urban systems lack many of the qualitative elements of successful systems, which put the systems under severe stress. South African society at large is expecting the urban systems to allocate values and be successful in sustaining that function but that very same society lacks the will to accept the allocations as binding. **2. Dynamic Response Model of an Urban System:** From what has been explained above, it is clear that the urban system also needs description in terms of a dynamic response or flow model. Such a model not only illustrates the fact that the system allows for the implementation of plans, but also sensitizes people to the fact that what it does may dynamically influence each successive stage of behaviour.

2.7.5. Principles of Balanced Application of All Criteria

The hypothesis presented is that of democratic and efficient restructuring of local government, the following principles should be taken into account:

1. The principle of good government: restructuring should enhance and assist governance;

2. The principle of megapolitics: restructuring should take cognizance of trends with respect to the shift of power from a central to a decentralized base;

3. The principles defined in the Constitution of the Country, and Local Government Act as well as the requirements of the statutory framework;

4. The demands, forces and realities of the modern African countries' urban environment;

5. The socio-political dimension: addressing the real needs and expectations of the people and emphasizing the system dynamics; and

6. The principle balance: the variety of important criteria and principles of demarcation should be applied in a balanced way.

This section has presented important principles and perspectives that should be taken into account when considering the restructuring of local government.

CHAPTER
THREE

LOCAL GOVERNMENT
IN DIFFERENT POLITICAL SYSTEMS

3.1. Introduction

Characteristics and types of local government differ from a country to the other. Most of the states have at least two tiers of local government, such as counties and municipalities. In some states, counties are divided into townships. There are several different types of jurisdictions at the municipal level, including the city, town, borough, and village.

Although there are special bodies for local government, for example, school boards in the United States of America, more important are those that carry out a broad range of public activities within a defined area and population. Almost all such local government bodies share certain characteristics: a continuing organization; the authority to undertake public activities; the ability to enter into contracts; the right to sue and be sued; and the ability to collect taxes and determine a budget. Areas of local government authority usually include public schools, local highways, municipal services, and some aspects of social welfare and public order. An important distinction among types of local government is that between representative bodies, which are elected locally and have decision-making authority, and non representative bodies, which are either appointed from above or, if elected locally, have no independent governing authority.

3.2. Categorization of Local Government in Different Political Systems

Local government can be categorized according to the way it is practiced in different political systems. The features that could be examined embrace structure, functions and operations. The variations may be the result of differences in political and administrative systems being practiced by those countries.

Local government system is practiced in three types of the political systems over the world. There is unitary system, the federal system, and the post-colonial systems in Africa.

3.2.1. Local Government Administration in the Unitary State

Local government administration in the unitary state system involves countries that have the principle of democracy and participation of citizens. There are two variations that are practiced by Britain and the other by France.

The major characteristics of these systems are:

1. It is either single or two tier system. For example, in Britain counties and districts are divided into metropolitan counties and non-metropolitan counties; metropolitan districts and

non-metropolitan districts. This is to distinguish between cities from the rural areas.

2. There is distribution of powers between the central government and local government. In the distribution of authority there is a great autonomy for local government units.
3. There is responsibility for the decision-making which is authority in powers and is vested in elected councilors. The councilors are the policy-making body.
4. The system highly depends on the committee structure which is responsible for policy-making as a domain of the elected councilors.
5. Policy implementation is the domain of the executive personnel.
6. Separation of powers between the elected council and the appointed/selected officials.
7. Authority is delegated by warrant to local authorities. The warrant contains powers and functions delegated to the local authority. Powers may be exercised independently at the county or district level.
8. Counties/districts are sub-divided into electoral wards where councilors are elected to the county/district councils. The councilors elect the mayor and the chairmen of the committees.
9. Local government units are corporate bodies and shoulder the responsibility before the electorates and protect the administration.

While most countries have complex systems of local government, those of France and Great Britain have served as models for much of the rest of the world. These models are as hereunder.

3.2.2. The French System of Local Government
3.2.2.1. Introduction
The French system of local government is among the most non representative system of local government. Its basic structure, codified by Napoleon I, developed out of the need of revolutionary France to curtail the power of local notables, while hastening government reform. It stresses clear lines of authority, reaching from the central government's ministry of the interior through the centrally appointed prefect of the department to the municipality, which has a locally elected mayor and municipal council. The prefect, being both the chief executive of the department and the representative of the central bureaucracy, provides the channel of centralization, with wide authority to overrule local councils and supervise local expenditures. Variants of this system are found throughout Europe and in former French colonies.

The French Constitution of 1958 combines parliamentary democracy and a presidential system, with separation of powers:

1. **Executive Power**: is shared between the President of the Republic and Prime Minister and his Government. The Government is responsible to Parliament.

2. **Legislative Power**: is exercised by Parliament (National assembly and senate).

3. **Judicial Power**: independent of the executive as well as of the legislative power, is exercised by the Courts.

3.2.2.2. The Political Organization of the State
The political organization of France is as hereunder:

1. **The President of the Republic**: is the Head of the State; he is elected for five years by universal suffrage.

2. **The Prime Minister**: is appointed by the President who is

the Head of the Government. The ministers, members of the Government, are appointed by the President on nomination by the prime Minister. The Government decides and conducts the national policy.

3. **Parliamen**t: exercises the legislative power, it consists of two houses:

a. a. The National assembly which has 577 deputies elected by direct suffrage for five years.

b. b. The Senate has 321 senators elected by indirect suffrage for nine years.

Apart from these traditional executive and legislative bodies several state institutions fulfill a judicial or advisory role as follows:

1. **The Constitutional Council**: ensures the regularity of elections and laws that conform to the Constitution.

2. **The Council of State**: Supreme Court for administrative matters.

3. **The Audit Court**: Authority charged with the audit of public accounts.

4. **The Higher Judicial Council**: Advisory body, guardian of the independence of the judiciary.

5. **The Economic and Social Committee**: Has an advisory role. It gives its opinion, at the government's request, on bills, draft ordinances and decrees. It is composed of a cross section of French Society, including those from the private sector.

3.2.2.3. Local Government

France, under the 1982 decentralization laws, has three tiers of local administration: communes, departments and regions.

1. The Commune

The commune is the simplest and oldest local administrative unit dating back to the parishes and cities of the Middle Ages, the commune was instituted in 1789. It was given a certain amount of autonomy under the Government Act of April 5th, 1884.

Although the commune varied in size, all communes share the same set of institutions with a municipal council elected for six years, under universal suffrage and a mayor elected by his peers within the council.

The mayor performs the executive functions of the commune. He sets and implements its policy and budget, and employs the local staff. He also represents the State in three areas: registry office, law and order, and the organization of elections.

The communes are responsible for local services such as:[18]

a. Town planning and development policy;

b. primary schools;

c. social welfare (responsibility shared with the department);

d. roads and streets;

e. school transport;

f. refuse collection; and

g. water supply and sewage.

In 2004, there were 36,763 communes in France (32,000 have less than 2,000 inhabitants, among them 22,000 have less than 500 inhabitants).

2. The Department

Dating back to the Revolution, the department had its powers increased through an elected assembly (the general council) under

---

18   Ministry of Interior, Local Government in France. The French Political and Administrative System.

the Government Act of August 10th, 1871. The prefect performed
the executive functions of the department until the Decentralization
Law of 1982 was passed, which transferred executive responsibilities from the prefect to the President of the General Council.

The general council is elected for six years under direct suffrage.
The president is elected from among its members. The president
draws up and implements the budget passed by the council. He is
in charge of the administration of the department.

Departments are in charge of a wide range of services as
hereunder:

a. Social welfare concerning the elderly, the handicapped, the
    underprivileged, and children suffering from abuse or neglect;
b. departmental roads (building and maintenance);
c. education: construction and maintenance of secondary schools
    (but curriculum, training and appointment of the teachers
    remains the State's responsibility); and
d. school transport throughout the department.

There are 100 departments of which 4 are overseas. Their
populations range from 70,000 to 1.5 million.[19]

3. The Region

The regions are the newest administrative units which were created
by the government in 1959 for economic planning. Through the
decentralization process of 1982, they became autonomous entities
with an elected assembly and specific powers. The first regional
assembly was elected in 1986 for six years under universal suffrage.

The president of the regional council is elected by the members
of the regional council. As in the other tiers of local government,

---

19   Ibid.

the president of the regional council is in charge of the administration and the staff employed by the regional council.

The council votes on the budget, the president draws it up, and they both implement it. Regions are responsible for:

a. Economic planning and development;
b. building and maintenance of general and technical high schools; and
c. technical training.

There are 26 regions (4 overseas) often corresponding to former provinces, although some are artificial entities.[20]

3.2.2.4. Prefects

The office of 'prefect' is unique in France. He is a civil servant, appointed by the President on nomination of the Prime Minister and the Minister of Interior to represent the State.

He embodies the power and authority of the State in the region or department he oversees. As such he has authority over all State employees in the region or department. He is locally responsible for:

a. Maintenance of law and order;
b. organization of elections;
c. organization of emergency and disaster relief;
d. administration of legislation and new policies enacted by the Government; and
e. supervision over the administration of law (legal review).

The prefect plays an important part in establishing contracts between the State and each region on economic planning: he

---

20   Ibid.

officiates and signs on behalf of the State as main negotiator. He plays a supporting role with respect to investment and economic projects.

Beyond these official responsibilities, the prefect coordinates different authorities to promote economic development and acts as mediator at the regional level in industrial disputes and demonstrations.

He is assisted in his task by a sub prefect in every district of the department.

The prefect of the department in which the regional centre is located acts as both departmental and regional prefect.

3.2.2.5. Legal Control

The decentralization laws put an end to the prefect's prior power to approve beforehand decisions taken by local authorities. They established a mechanism of control based on three principles:

1. Local Authorities' decisions come into force immediately after being published, notified, or for some specific decisions, transmitted to the prefect.
2. The prefect's supervision only concerns the legal aspect of the decision once adopted (post hoc control).
3. The State representative has no power to invalidate a measure taken by a local authority he considers illegal; he must refer it to an administrative court, which has the power to invalidate it if necessary.

In addition to the representative of the State, any concerned party can refer a local decision before an administrative court.

3.2.2.6. The Principles of Local Government in France

Decentralization has been carried out since 1982 in accordance with the following principles:

1. Reduction of administrative supervision by the prefects.
2. Transfer of executive power to the heads of the elected bodies' at all three levels.
3. Creation of regions as full local authorities with elected councils, similar to departments and communes.
4. Progressive transfer of State responsibilities to the three levels of local authority as well as corresponding staff and financial means to meet the new responsibilities and charges.
5. Full autonomy of local authorities within their sphere of responsibility. There is no hierarchy or supervision between the different levels of local authority.
6. Creation of a specific statute governing the employment of the local authority staff.

3.2.3. The British System of Local Government
3.2.3.1. Introduction

The United Kingdom is the union between the nations of England, Scotland, Wales and Northern Ireland. The proper definition is "the United Kingdom of Great Britain and Northern Ireland" but this is shortened to "the United Kingdom", "Great Britain" or just "UK". [21]

The British system of local government, which has been the model for most of the country's former colonies, including the United States, is the most representative of the major types. Largely reformed in the 19th century and extensively restructured in the 1970s. The system stresses local government autonomy through elected councils on the county and sub county levels. This system

---

21   Michela Giordano, Local Government in the United Kingdom. Internet.

was marked by less central government interference and greater local budgetary authority than in other systems. However, in 1986, six major county governments were abolished by Parliament, while the powers of others were restricted. A special feature of the British system is its use of an extensive committee system, instead of a strong executive, for supervising the administration of public services.[22]

3.2.3.2.History of Local Government in England

In England, during the Anglo-Saxon period, *shires* were areas used for the raising of taxes, and usually had a fortified town at their centre. These became known as the shire town or the county town. The name 'county' was introduced by the Normans, and was derived from a Norman term for an area administered by a Count (lord). These Norman 'counties' were geographically based upon the Saxon shires, and kept their Saxon names.

In the Medieval period, county boundaries of England were changed over time. It was the time that a number of important cities were granted the status of counties, such as London, Bristol and Coventry. For centuries, the counties were used mainly for legal administration and tax raising. In 1889 administrative counties (county councils) were created and they were based upon the tradi-tional county areas.

The first local government districts were created in 1894 by the Local Government Act 1894 which created Urban districts and rural districts as sub-divisions of administrative counties (which had been created in 1889). Another reform in 1899 created 28 metro-politan boroughs as sub-divisions of the County of London.

In 1965 and 1974 a major re-organisation of local government created several new administrative counties and also created several

---

22   Ibid.

new metropolitan counties. In 1965 Greater London and its 32 London boroughs were created. They are the oldest type of district still in use.

In 1974, the administrative counties were abolished and Metropolitan counties and Non-metropolitan counties (or 'Shire counties') were created across the rest of England and were split into Metropolitan districts and Non-metropolitan districts. The metropolitan and non-metropolitan counties replaced the system of administrative counties which were introduced in 1889.

The status of the London boroughs and metropolitan districts changed in 1986. They absorbed the functions and some of the powers of the metropolitan county councils and the Greater London Council which were abolished. In London, power is now shared again, on a different basis, with the Greater London Authority

During the 1990s a further kind of district was created, the unitary authority, which combined the functions and status of county and district.

County was derived from the French word '*comté*' which was simply used by the Normans after 1066 to replace the native English term *scir* which means in Modern English '*shire*'. A shire was an administrative division of an Anglo-Saxon kingdom (Wessex, Mercia, East Anglia), usually named after its administrative centre (Gloucester, in Gloucestershire; Worcester, in Worcestershire). Many of the names of British Counties are suffixed by the word "shire" that was once controlled on behalf of the sovereign by a 'Shire Reeve' or Sheriff.[23]

Counties in England were originally based on the traditional counties of England. County level local authorities (county councils) in the UK are responsible for running education, libraries,

---

23   Ibid.

waste disposal, highways and transport, strategic land use, emergency services, planning, social services, and a number of other functions.

3.2.3.3. Systems of Local Government in UK
There are two common systems of local government in the UK and they are:[24]
1. The old-style two-tier system
The older two-tier system consists of:
a. District Councils responsible for rubbish collection, granting planning permission and council housing, leisure, local roads, and environmental health.
b. County Councils responsible for education, social services, libraries, main roads, trading standards, some public transport and other local functions.

2. The newer single-tier system
The newer single-tier system consists of:
a. Unitary Authorities: have a single-tier system (only one level) of local government, and combine District and County Council functions into one body.
b. In Greater London, a unique two-tier system exists, with power shared between the London borough councils, and the Greater London Authority which is headed by an elected Mayor.

3.2.3.4. Administrative Divisions of Local Government in England
For the purposes of local government, England is divided into four levels of administrative divisions as in table 3.1:

---

24   Ibid.

Table 3.1 Shows Administrative Divisions of England

1) Regional Level	
2) County Level	Metropolitan County Shire County Unitary Authority Greater London
3) District Level	Metropolitan District Non- Metropolitan District London borough
4) Parish Level	Civil Parish

Source: Michela Giordano,
Local Government in the United Kingdom. Internet.

3.2.3.5. Regions in England
England is divided into nine regions. The regions were created in 1994. Since the 1999 Euro-elections, they have been used as England's European Parliament constituencies. The regions vary greatly in size, both in their areas and their populations. The region is currently the highest tier (level) of local government in the United Kingdom.

3.2.3.6. Sub-divisions of the Regions
Local government in England does not follow a uniform structure. Each region is divided into a range of further sub divisions: the layers of government below the regions are mixed.
1. Greater London is divided into 32 London boroughs and the City of London.
2. The other regions are divided into metropolitan counties, shire counties and unitary authorities.

Counties are further divided into districts and in some areas there are also parishes.

3.2.3.7. England's Local Government Units at County Level

The units of local government at county level in England are as follows:[25]

1. **Metropolitan counties**: There are six metropolitan counties, divided into metropolitan districts, which cover large urban areas outside London. They were created in 1974. In 1986 their county councils were abolished.

2. **Non-metropolitan or shire counties**: Shire counties or non–metropolitan counties were also created in 1974. They are 34 and they are divided into non-metropolitan districts. They cover much of the country, though mainly the rural areas.

3. **Unitary authorities**: Unitary authorities were created in the 1990s and are single-tier authorities which combine the functions of county and district councils. There are 47 of them. A unitary authority is responsible for all local government functions within its area. This is opposed to a two-tier system where local government functions are divided between different authorities. Typically unitary authorities cover large towns or cities.

4. **Greater London**: Greater London was created in 1965 and it is divided into the City of London and 32 London Boroughs. The term "London" is often used in reference to Greater London. Greater London originally had a two-tier system of local government: the Greater London Council (GLC) shared power with the Corporation of London (governing the small City of London) and the 32 London borough councils. The Greater London Council was abolished in 1986.

---

25   Ibid.

The tiny City of London at its centre is often called "the City" or "the Square Mile" and forms the main financial district. London is the only English region with a directly elected mayor and an elected regional assembly which together comprise the Greater London Authority (the "GLA"), which oversees transport, the fire brigade and economic development.

3.2.3.8. England's Units of Local Government at District level

There are four units of local government at district level in England and they are as follows:

1. The term 'District' can have a number of different meanings: in general, it refers to an administrative area with its own elected council.

2. Some districts are styled as boroughs, cities, or royal boroughs. These are honorific titles, and do not alter the status of the district.

3. All Boroughs and Cities, and a very few Districts, are led by a Mayor elected by the Council: in most cases, it is a ceremonial role.

4. After the most recent local government reform, the mayor is a directly elected_Mayor: he/she takes most of the policy decisions instead of the Council.

3.2.3.9. Metropolitan district

Metropolitan districts or metropolitan boroughs are a subdivision of a metropolitan county. When the county councils were abolished in 1986, most of the powers of the county councils were devolved to the metropolitan districts which therefore function similar to other unitary authorities. The districts typically have populations of 174,000 to 1.1 million.

3.2.3.10. Non-metropolitan (shire) district

Shire counties are divided into non-metropolitan districts. Non-metropolitan districts (shire districts) are second-tier authorities, which share power with county councils. They are subdivisions of shire counties and the most common type of district. The districts typically have populations of 25,000 to 200,000. The number of non-metropolitan districts has varied over time.

3.2.3.11. London Boroughs

The 32 London borough councils have a similar status to other unitary authorities. They run most of the day-to-day services across the capital. Each council is made up of elected councillors. They set the Council Tax levels which, along with extra funding from central government, allows each borough to provide services such as education, housing, social services, street cleaning, waste disposal, roads, local planning and many arts and leisure services. The boroughs do not run police or health services.

3.2.3.12. Civil Parish Level

Below the district level, a district may be divided into several civil parishes. The civil parish is the most local unit of government in England. Civil parishes are usually administered by parish councils, which have various local responsibilities. A parish council can also be called a town council or occasionally a city council. The chair of a town council or city council will usually have the title of Mayor.

The Parish is the lowest level of local government formed at a time when there was little difference, to the local people, between the Church and the State.

The parish is usually formed around a village or other small community and used to be centred around the Parish Church.

Parishes are known as 'local councils'. The role played by parish councils varies. Smaller parish councils have only limited resources and generally play only a minor role. Some larger parish councils have a role similar to that of a small district council. Parish councils receive funding from the council tax paid by the residents of the parish.

3.2.3.13. Activities of Parish Councils
Activities undertaken by parish or town councils include:
1. Provision of certain local facilities such as allotments, bus shelters, parks, playgrounds, public seats, public toilets, public clocks, street lights, village or town halls, leisure and recreation facilities.
2. Maintenance of footpaths, cemeteries and village greens.
3. Provision of community transport (such as a minibus), crime prevention measures.
4. Giving of grants to local voluntary organizations, and sponsoring public events, including entering Britain in Bloom.
5. Parish councils have the right to be consulted on any planning decisions affecting the parish.

3.2.3.14. Local Councils
Local government authorities (known as councils) have powers because the central government has given them powers. The system of local government is very similar to the system of national government. There are elected representatives (called councillors) who meet in a council chamber in the Town Hall or County Hall. Local councils traditionally manage nearly all public services. Local councils are allowed to collect a tax called the "council tax". It is based on the estimated value of a property and the number of people living in it.

3.2.3.15. Single-tier Local Government Services
Single-tier authorities are responsible for:
1. Education;
2. social services and housing;
3. council tax benefits;
4. public libraries;
5. museums and art galleries;
6. traffic and transportation;
7. refuse collection, recycling and disposal;
8. planning;
9. environmental health;
10. swimming pools;
11. leisure facilities;
12. parks;
13. open spaces;
14. countryside including footpaths;
15. cemeteries and crematoria;
16. markets and fairs;
17. registration of births, deaths, marriages and electorates; and
18. collecting council tax and business rates.

3.2.3.16. Multiple-tier Local Government Services
Multiple-tier authorities are as in table 3.2 below.

Table 3.2 Shows Spheres of Responsibilities of the County, District and Town/Parish Councils

County Councils	District Councils	Town and Parish Councils
1. education 2. libraries 3. social services 4. trading, standards 5. waste disposal 6. highways and transport 7. strategic land use 8. planning	1. housing 2. parks 3. sports 4. arts and entertainment 5. land 6. use planning permission 7. environmental health 8. waste collection and recycling 9. street cleaning 10. council tax collection 11. council tax and housing 12. electoral registration and administration	1. community centres 2. arts and leisure facilities 3. parks and play areas 4. public conveniences and other services 5. have a right to be notified about planning in the area.

Source: Michela Giordano, Local Government in the United Kingdom.
Internet.

3.3. Local Government in the Federal System

Federal states have two hierarchies of decentralization. The middle layer is either a state or regional government which exercises particular functions. In spite of states or regions, authority is vested in the local government organizations which are at the bottom of the hierarchy.

In the federal states system, development activities are given to the local government and are allowed a degree of autonomy. Powers are devolved to the local government.

Despite differences among states, local governments of the United States follow the general principles of the British system, except that a strong executive is common. The county remains the usual political subdivision, although it has retained more authority in rural than in urban areas, where incorporated municipalities have most of the local power. In both rural and urban areas the local government's relationship to the state is a complex one of shared authority and carefully defined areas of legal competence. Local governments are pulled two ways, increasingly reliant on state and federal funding to carry out their expected duties, while fearful of losing their traditional degree of local control.

In the USA, local government is the responsibility of the State government. There are three identified systems:

a. **Strong Mayor System:** A city Mayor is elected by citizens and is entrusted with the administration of the city. The Mayor is assisted by the elected councilors who elect the heads of the departments who in turn form the administration arm of the city. The decision-making is entrusted to the Mayor.

b. **Councilors:** The councilors are elected who in turn elect the mayor. Authority is exercised by the councilors who determine policy matters. The executive organ is entrusted with the day-to-day administration of services.

c. **City Manager System:** Executive officer is selected and is a person who has skills and experience in the management of services. He is given authority to decide on issues on the basis of technical competence and feasibility. He may be advised by the committees of councilors but his decisions are overriding/take precedence.

3.4. Local Government in the Post-colonial Systems in the Third World Countries
3.4.1. Introduction
In the newly independent states of Africa and Asia, local government administration underwent a serious of re-examination in the post-colonial era. In some countries review has been prompted by the fact that the newly independent states could not afford to run the local government system. Some countries abandoned the system of local government administration and in favor adapted other traditionally based administrative institutions, for example, Tanzania adapted Ujamaa Movement.

3.4.2. Meaning of Ujamaa
Ujamaa is the Swahili word for extended family. It was a social and economic policy developed and implemented in Tanzania by President Julius Kambarage Nyerere (1922–1999) between 1964 and 1985. Based on the idea of collective farming and the «Villagization" of the countryside, Ujamaa also called for the nationalization of banks and industry and an increased level of self-reliance at both at an individual and national level.[26]

---

26   Internet.

3.4.3. Nyerere's Plan of Ujamaa

Nyerere argued that urbanization, which had been brought about by European colonialism and was economically driven by wage labor, had disrupted the traditional pre-colonial rural African society. He believed that it was possible for his government to recreate pre-colonial traditions in Tanzania and, in turn, re-establish a traditional level of mutual respect and return the people to settled, moral ways of life. The main way to do that, he said, was to move people out of the urban cities like the capital Dar es Salaam and into newly created villages dotting the rural countryside.

The idea for collective rural agriculture seemed like a sound idea—Nyerere's government could afford to provide equipment, facilities, and material to a rural population if they were brought together in "nucleated" settlements, each of around 250 families. Establishing new groups of rural populations also made the distribution of fertilizer and seed easier, and it would be possible to provide a good level of education to the population as well. Villagization was seen as a way to overcome the problems of "tribalization"—a plague which beset other newly independent African countries that drove people to separate into tribes based on ancient identities.

Nyerere set out his policy in the Arusha Declaration of February 5, 1967. The process started slowly and was voluntary at first, but by the end of the 1960s, there were only 800 or so collective settlements. In the 1970s, Nyerere's reign became more oppressive, as he began to force people to leave the cities and move to the collective villages. By the end of the 1970s, there were over 2,500 of these villages: but things weren't going well in them.[27]

---

27   Ibid.

3.4.4. Weaknesses of Ujamaa Policy

Ujamaa was intended to recreate nuclear families and engage the small communities in an "economy of affection" by tapping into the traditional African attitudes, while at the same time introducing essential services and modern technological innovations for the rural population that was now the majority. But traditional ideals of how families operated no longer matched the reality of the Tanzanians. The traditional devoted female domestic guardian of the family rooted in the village was contrary to the actual lifestyles of women—and may be the ideal never had worked. Instead, women moved in and out of working and raising children throughout their lives, embracing diversification and flexibility to provide personal security.

At the same time, although young men complied with the official orders and moved to the rural communities, they rejected the traditional models and distanced themselves from the older generation of male leaders within their family.

According to a 2014 survey of people living in Dar el Salaam, Villagization did not provide enough economic incentive to people who had been used to wage labor. They found themselves needing to involve themselves ever more deeply in the urban/wage economy. Ironically, Ujamaa villagers resisted engaging in communal life and withdrew from subsistence and commercial agriculture, while urban residents chose to live in the cities and practice urban agriculture.[28]

3.4.5. Failure of Ujamaa

Nyerere's socialist outlook required Tanzania's leaders to reject capitalism and all its trimmings, showing restraint over salaries and other perks. But as the policy was rejected by a significant fraction

---

28   Ibid.

of the population, the main foundation of Ujamaa, Villagization, failed. Productivity was supposed to be increased through collectivization; instead, it fell to less than 50% of what had been achieved on independent farms. Toward the end of Nyerere's rule, Tanzania had become one of Africa's poorest countries, dependent on international aid.

Ujamaa was brought to an end in 1985 when Nyerere stepped down from the Presidency in favor of Ali Hassan Mwinyi.[29]

3.4.6. Advantages of Ujamaa

The advantages of Ujamaa were as follows:[30]

a. Created a high literacy rate.
b. Halved infant mortality through access to medical facilities and education.
c. United Tanzanians across ethnic lines.
d. Left Tanzania untouched by the "tribal" and political tensions that affected the rest of Africa

3.4.7. Disadvantages of Ujamaa

The disadvantages of Ujamaa were as hereunder:[31]

a. Transportation networks declined drastically through neglect.
b. Industry and banking were crippled.
c. Left the country dependent on international aid.

3.5. Indian System of Local Government
3.5.1. Introduction

The Indian system of local government is built on the concept of community development organization. Local government units

---

29   Ibid.
30   Ibid.
31   Ibid.

are known as Community Development Blocks. Each block has a population of 60,000-80,000 in the urban areas, and 20,000-30,000 in the rural areas. Responsibility includes sectors of agriculture, animal husbandry, rural engineering, social education, cooperatives, rural industries and primary health. These seven officers responsible for the sectors advise Block Development Officers.

Local government in India refers to governmental jurisdictions below the level of the state. India is a federal republic with three spheres of government: central, state and local.

The 73rd and 74th constitutional amendments give recognition and protection to local governments and in addition each state has its own local government legislation.[32] Since 1992, local government in India takes place in two very distinct forms. Urban localities, covered in the 74th amendment to the Constitution,[33] have Nagar Palika but derive their powers from the individual state governments, while the powers of rural localities have been formalized under the Panchayati Raj System (PRS), under the 73rd amendment to the Constitution.[34]

For the history of traditional local government Councils of India (zilla parishads) at the district level, 6,672 were panchayat samitis at the block level, and 255,466 were gram Panchayats at the village level.

The Panchayati Raj System is a three-tier system with elected bodies at the village, taluk and district levels. The modern system is based in part on traditional (Panchayati Raj, Panchayat governance), in part on the vision of Mahatma Gandhi and in part by the work of various committees to harmonize the highly centralized Indian

---

32   "The Local Government System in India" (PDF). Commonwealth Local Government Forum.

33   The Constitution (Seventy-fourth Amendment) Act, 1992

34   The Constitution (Seventy-third Amendment) Act, 1992

governmental administration with a degree of local autonomy.[35]
The result was intended to create greater participation in local government by people and more effective implementation of rural development programs. Although, as of 2015, implementation in all of India is not complete, the intention is for there to be a gram panchayat for each village or group of villages, a tehsil level council, and a zilla panchayat at the district level.

3.5.2. Rural Local Governments in India
Rural local governments or panchayat raj institutions[36] (PRIs) are as the following:
1. Zilla panchayats;
2. Mandal or taluka panchayats; and
3. Gram panchayats.

The Constitution of India visualizes panchayats as institutions of self-governance. However, giving due consideration to the federal structure of India's polity, most of the financial powers and authorities to be endowed on panchayats have been left at the discretion of concerned state legislatures. Consequently, the powers and functions vested in PRIs vary from state to state. These provisions combine representative and direct democracy into a synergy and are expected to result in an extension and deepening of democracy in India. Hence, panchayats have journeyed from an institution within the culture of India to attain constitutional status.

35   Singh,Vijandra (2003). "Chapter 5: Panchayati Raj and Gandhi". Panchayati Raj andVillage Development:Volume 3, Perspectives on Panchayati Raj Administration. Studies in public administration. New Delhi: Sarup & Sons. pp. 84–90. ISBN 978-81-7625-392-5.
36   "The Local Government System in India" (PDF). Commonwealth Local Government Forum.

3.5.3. Functions of Municipal Government in India

All municipal acts in India provide for functions, powers and responsibilities to be carried out by the municipal government. These are divided into two categories: obligatory and discretionary.

3.5.3.1. Obligatory Functions

The obligatory functions are as follows:

1. supply of pure and wholesome water;
2. construction and maintenance of public streets;
3. lighting and watering of public streets;
4. cleaning of public streets, places and sewers;
5. regulation of offensive, dangerous or obnoxious trades and callings or practices;
6. maintenance or support of public hospitals;
7. establishment and maintenance of primary schools;
8. registration of births and deaths;
9. removing obstructions and projections in public streets, bridges and other places;
10. naming streets and numbering houses; and
11. maintenance of law and public order.

3.5.3.2. Discretionary Functions

Discretionary functions are as follows:

1. laying out of areas;
2. securing or removal of dangerous buildings or places;
3. construction and maintenance of public parks, gardens, libraries, museums, rest houses, leper homes, orphanages and rescue homes for women;
4. public buildings;
5. planting of trees and maintenance of roads;

6. housing for low income groups;
7. conducting surveys;
8. organizing public receptions, public exhibitions, public entertainment;
9. provision of transport facilities with the municipality; and
10. promotion of welfare of municipal employees.

Some of the functions of the urban bodies overlap with the work of state agencies. The functions of the municipality, including those listed in the Twelfth Schedule to the Constitution, are left to the discretion of the state government. Local bodies have to be bestowed with adequate powers, authority and responsibility to perform the functions entrusted to them by the Act.

It is worthy to mention that in some countries in the Third World, local government system was continued just as it was introduced by the colonizers. In other countries, it was also maintained as a fashionable practice of democracy or because it is a form of administrative exercise of a modern state.

Local government on the whole in the under developed countries suffers because of poverty. This situation is aggravated by the population explosion and the growth of the shanty towns.[37]

---

37   Internet.

CHAPTER FOUR

GOOD GOVERNANCE

4.1. Introduction

The terms "governance" and "good governance" are being increasingly used in development literature. Bad governance is being increasingly regarded as one of the root causes of all evil within our societies. Major donors and international financial institutions are increasingly basing their aid and loans on the condition that reforms that ensure "good governance" are undertaken.[38]

4.2. Meaning of Governance and Good Governance
4.2.1. Governance

The concept of "governance" is not new. It is as old as human civilization. Simply put "governance" means: "the process of decision-making and the process by which decisions are implemented or not implemented."[39] Governance in this context can

---

38   Internet.
39   Ibid.

apply to corporate, international, national, or local governance[40] as well as the interactions between other sectors of society.

Since governance is the process of decision making and process by which decisions are implemented, an analysis of governance focuses on the formal and informal actors involved in decision making and implementing the decisions made and the formal and informal structures that have been set in place to arrive at and implement the decision.

Government is one of the actors in governance. Other actors involved in governance vary depending on the level of government that is under discussions. In rural areas, for example, other actors may include influential landlords, associations of peasant farmers, cooperatives, NGOs, research institutes, religious leaders, finance institutions, political parties, the military etc. The situation in the urban areas is much more complex where there are interconnections between actors, media, lobbyists, international donors, multi-national corporations, etc., who may play a role in decision making or influencing the decision making process. All actors other than government and the military are grouped together as part of the civil society, organized crime syndicates also influence decision making, particularly in urban areas and at the national level.

Similarly formal government structures are one means by which decisions are arrived at and implemented. At the national level, informal decision making structure, such as "kitchen cabinets" or informal advisors may exist. In urban areas, organized crime syndicates such as the "land mafia" may influence the decision making. In some rural areas locally powerful families may make or influence decision making. Such, informal decision making is often the result of corrupt practices or leads to corrupt practices.

---

40   Ibid.

Governance is the system and process of ensuring the direction, supervision and accountability of an organization. Governance does not have to be completed, and is equally important for organizations of all sizes. Governance is not just about compliance, structure and duties. Governance is often viewed as a compliance task. Governance should be viewed as a journey and something that is never truly completed.

Governance can be defined as: "The system by which entities are directed and controlled. It is concerned with structure and processes for decision making, accountability, control and behaviour at the top of an entity. Governance influences how an organization's objectives are set and achieved, how risk is monitored and addressed and how performance is optimized". Governance is a system and process, not a single activity and therefore successful implementation of a good governance strategy requires a systematic approach that incorporates strategic planning, risk management and performance management. Like culture, it is a core component of the unique characteristics of a successful organization.

4.2.2. Good Governance

The concept of "good governance" emerges as a model to compare ineffective economies or political bodies with viable economies and political bodies.[41] The concept centres on the responsibility of governments and governing bodies to meet the needs of the masses as opposed to select groups in society. Because countries often described as "most successful" are liberal democratic states, concentrated in Europe and the Americas, good governance

---

41   Khan, Mushtaq Husain (2004). State formation in Palestine: viability and governance during a social transformation: Volume 2 of Political economy of the Middle East and North Africa. Routledge. ISBN 978-0-415-33802-8. found at Google Books

standards often measure other state institutions against these states.[42] Aid organizations and the authorities of developed countries often will focus the meaning of «good governance» to a set of requirements that conform to the organization's agenda, making *good governance* imply many different things in many different contexts.[43]

Good governance is an indeterminate term used in the international development literature to describe how public institutions conduct public affairs and manage public resources. Good governance is crucial to an organization's success and is not something to be feared. In social enterprise, that success has an impact on the communities in which it operates.

In international development, good governance is a way of measuring how public institutions conduct public affairs and manage public resources in a preferred way.

4.3. Importance of Good Governance

The fundamental reasons why organizations should adopt good governance practices include:

1. To preserve and strengthen stakeholder confidence–nothing distracts an organization more than having to deal with a disgruntled stakeholder group caused by a lack of confidence in the governing body. And on the positive side, a supportive stakeholder base can generate benefits for the organization though social and emotional support, intangible but very valuable attributes that all organizations should strive to achieve and sustain;

2. To provide the foundation for a high-performing organization–the achievement of goals and sustainable success requires

---

42   Ibid.
43   Agere 1, Agere 4, Poluha, Eva; Rosendahl, Mona (2002). Contesting 'good' governance:crosscultural perspectives on representation, accountability and public space. Routledge. ISBN 978-0-7007-1494-0

input and support from all levels of an organization. The Board, though it has good governance practices, provides the framework for planning, implementation and monitoring of performance and without a foundation on which it can build high performance upon, the achievement of this goal becomes problematic. Achievement of the best performance and results possible, within existing capacity and capability, should be an organization's ongoing goal. Good governance should support management and staff to be "the best they can be"; and

3. To ensure that the organization is well placed to respond to a changing external environment–government or business today operates in an environment of constant change. Technology has created an information age that has transformed our world, and for business to both survive and remain profitable to enable it to fulfill its mission and achieve its vision, a system has to be in place to assist an organization to identify changes in both the external environment and emerging trends. This process of understanding our changing world does not happen by chance, it requires leadership, commitment and resources from the governing body to establish and maintain such a system within the organization. Change generally does not happen "over-night", it is there for all to see if they have in place a system for looking. Governing bodies, as the ultimate leaders of an organization, should take prime responsibility for this activity.

In summary, governance encompasses the processes by which organizations are directed, controlled and held to account. It includes the authority, accountability, leadership, direction and control exercised in an organization. Greatness can be achieved when good governance principles and practices are applied throughout the whole organization and that's why governance is important.

4.4. Importance of Good Governance to Local Government

Good governance is argued to be the most important in local governments. It tries to promote more relationships between government and:

1. Empowered citizens.
2. Neighborhood councils.
3. Community councils.

Good governance with local government aims to increase civil engagement with more members of the community in order to get the best options that serves the people.[44]

4.5. Characteristics of Good Governance

The characteristics of good governance are also known as features or elements of good governance. Good governance has eight major characteristics. It is participatory, consensus oriented, accountable, transparent, responsive, effective and efficient, equitable and inclusive and follows the rule of law. These characteristics are as in figure 3.1.

Good governance assures that corruption is minimized, the views of minorities are taken into account and that the voices of the most vulnerable in society are heard in decision making. It is also responsive to the present and the future needs of society.

---

44   "A User's Guide to Measuring Local Governance" UNDP.

Figure 4.1 Diagram of the Characteristics of Good Governance

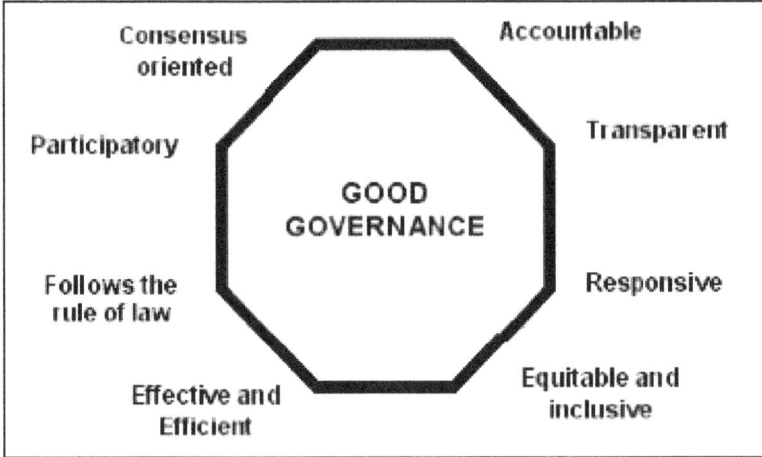

The characteristics of good governance are as the following:

1. **Participation**: Participation by both men and women is a key cornerstone of good governance. Participation could be either directed or through legitimate intermediate institutions or representatives. It is important to point out that representative democracy does not necessarily mean that concerns of the most vulnerable in society would be taken into consideration in decision making. Participation needs to be informed and organized. This means freedom of association and expression on the one hand and an organized civil society on the other hand.

2. **Rule of Law**: Good governance requires fair legal frameworks that are enforced impartially. It also requires full protection of human rights, particularly those of minorities. Impartial

enforcement of laws requires an independent judiciary and impartial and incompatible police force.

3. **Transparency**: Transparency means that decisions taken and their enforcement are done in a manner that follows rules and regulations. It also means that information is freely available and directly accessible to those who will be affected by such decisions and their enforcement. It also means that enough information is provided and that it is provided in an easily understandable forms and media.

4. **Responsiveness**: Good governance requires that institutions and processes try to serve all stakeholders within a reasonable timeframe.

5. **Consensus Oriented**: There are several actors and as many view points in a given society. Good governance requires mediation of the different interests in society on what is in the best interest of the whole community and how this can be achieved. It also requires a broad and long-term perspective on what is needed for sustainable human development and how to achieve the goals of such development. This can only result from an understanding of the historical, cultural and social contexts of a given society or community.

6. **Equity and Inclusiveness**: A society's wellbeing depends on ensuring that all its members feel that they have a stake in it and do not feel excluded from the mainstream of society. This requires all groups, but particularly the most vulnerable, have opportunities to improve or maintain their wellbeing.

7. **Effectiveness and Efficiency**: Good governance means that processes and institutions produce results that meet the needs of society while making the best use of resources at their disposal. The concept of efficiency in the context of good governance

also covers the sustainable use of natural resources and protection of the environment.

8. **Accountability**: Accountability is a key requirement of good governance. Not only governmental institutions but also the private sector and civil society organizations must be accountable to the public and their institutional stakeholders. Who is accountable to who varies depending on whether decisions or actions taken are internal or external to an organization or institution. In general an organization or an institution is accountable to those who will be affected by its decisions or actions. Accountability cannot be enforced without transparency and the rule of law.

From the discussion above, it can be concluded that it should be clear that good governance is an ideal which is difficult to achieve in its totality. Very few countries and societies have come close to achieving good governance in its totality. However, to ensure sustainable human development, actions must be taken to work towards this ideal with the aim of making it a reality.

4.6. Principles of Good Governance

Good governance is not an end by itself as it means the achieving of wider goals, such as social and political development, the alleviation of poverty, and the protection of the environment. Good government cannot be precisely defined. It is rather a set of ideas regarding the legitimacy, competence and accountability of government, about respect for human rights and the rule of law, which together add up to what most people expect from those who rule over them.

Good government is the essential framework within which business can flourish and provide economic prosperity, and ordinary citizens can seek to have their health, education and welfare needs met. Without good government, economic, social and political progress is difficult to achieve and impossible to guarantee.

There is no single blueprint for good government, only a set of principles that can be applied according to local circumstances. In an attempt to simplify responses to the above, the British Council explains the key elements of good government by stating that it (British Council, 1999: 18):

a. is accountable;

b. gives value of money;

c. is responsive;

d. is open;

e. observes standards;

f. offers information;

g. is fair;

h. observes rights;

i. is helpful; and

j. depends on consent.

Botha (1993: 25) defines local government as a mechanism for promotion of three fundamental values:

1. freedom by distributing political power and providing for local variation;

2. participation by providing choice and individual involvement; and

3. effectiveness and efficiency by being close to people and providing for unique local goals.

Important trends, often overlooked by local politicians and administrators, are the worldwide trends towards decentralization of activities and the privatization of government. The main forces behind privatization may be summarized as being that it is (Savas, 1987: 45).

1. **Pragmatic**: resulting in better government;
2. **Ideological**: the need for less government;
3. **Commercial**: more business and increasing global competitiveness; and
4. **Populist**: more choice in public services, and building a better society.

Another emerging principle is that of 'cities without boundaries' implying that for every function, there exists an optimal area of jurisdiction or functioning. Thus, the principles of good government can therefore be regarded as the following:

1. **Responsibility, Transparency, and Accountability**: Responsibility is an ongoing duty to complete the task at hand. Whereas transparency is where an organization must provide information about its activities and governance to stakeholders. The information should be accurate, complete and made available in a timely way. Transparency enables accountability. While accountability is literally the ability/or duty to report or give account on events, tasks, and experiences.

2. **Legitimacy and Authority**: Legitimacy denotes a system of government. An authority viewed as legitimate often has the right and justification to exercise power. It is the right and acceptance of an authority, usually a governing law or a regime. Whereas authority denotes a specific position in an established government. An authority is viewed as legitimate when often it has the right and justification to exercise power.

3. **Effectiveness and Efficiency**: Effectiveness is doing the right things. Whereas efficiency is performing or functioning in the

best possible manner with the least waste of time and effort. Efficiency is about doing things right.

4. **Economy of Scale**: Is the cost of the advantage reaped when production becomes efficient. Institutions can achieve economy of scale by increasing production and lowering cost. This happens because the cost is spread over a larger number of goods.

5. **Inclusivity**: Is the practice or policy of providing equal access to opportunities and resources for people who might otherwise be excluded or marginalized, such as those having physical or mental disabilities or belonging to other minority groups.

6. **Adherence to the Rule of law**: Is a principle of governance in which all persons, institutions and entities, public and private, including the State itself, are accountable to laws that are publicly promulgated, equally enforced and independently adjudicated, and which are consistent with international human rights, norms and standards.

7. **Sustainability and Consistency**: Sustainability is the ability of maintaining things at a certain rate or level. Whereas consistency is conformity in the application of something, typically that which is necessary for the sake of logic, accuracy or fairness.

8. **Financial Self-sufficiency**: Is the ratio that is used for the evaluation of the company's ability to generate revenue to cover its total costs while maintaining its equity value and other concession funds relative to the inflation and other cost of capital.

9. **Accessibility:** Is the quality of being able to be reached or entered. The quality of being easy to obtain or use. Moreover, it is the quality of being easily understood or appreciated.

10. **Respect for Individual Liberty**: Is the protection of the rights of others. Individual liberty is the liberty of those persons who are free from external restrain in the exercise of those rights which are considered to be outside the province of a government control.

11. **Community Involvement**: Is the power to bring positive, measurable change to both the communities in which you operate and to your business. It is moving closer to the core of what the company does.

12. **Responsiveness and Flexibility**: Responsiveness is the quality of reaching quickly and positively. Responsiveness is when some spontaneous event sets up a valuable learning opportunity; pause, acknowledge the outside content, and either adapt the lesson to it or address it enough to go back to the original plan. Whereas flexibility is when an institutional activity isn't working by modifying the activity, changing the pace, or backing up and explaining further. It is the quality of bending easily without breaking. It is the ability to be easily modified, or willingness to change or compromise.

13. **Empowerment and Reconstruction**: Empowerment is the authority or power given to someone to do something. It is the process of becoming stronger and more confident, especially in controlling one's life and claiming one's rights. Empowerment is the degree of autonomy and self-determination in people and in communities. This enables them to represent their interests in a responsible and self-determined way, acting on their own authority. Whereas reconstruction encompassed three major initiatives, restoration of the union, transformation and enactment of progressive legislation favoring of freedom. Reconstruction is the action or process of reconstructing or

being reconstructed. A thing that has been rebuilt after being damaged or destroyed. It embodies rebuilding, re-establishment, restoration, renovation, reintegration, reconstruction, instauration, and rehabilitation.

14. **Privatization, Decentralization and Devolution of Power**. Privatization is the transfer of business, industry, or service from public to private ownership and control. Whereas decentralization is the transfer of control of an activity or organization to several local offices or authorities rather than one single one. While devolution is the transfer or delegation of power to a lower level, especially by central government to local or regional administration.

A review of the above literature and inputs has resulted in the proposal that, for local government restructuring to be effective and efficient, the results should be tested against the principles of good government.

4.7. Practices of Good Governance

The Practices of good governance can be represented as seven Pillars, incorporating the following:

1. **Direction:** the institution has to be clear about the business they are operating, what they want to achieve and the type of values and principles that frame the way they do the business. The board is responsible for these key strategic issues and for proving leadership in establishing the right culture to drive the performance of the business. Without clear direction, the organization will flounder and likely never to realize its long term goals and potential.

2. **Viability & Sustainability:** a key priority in today's dynamic, ever changing environment. The institution is to be certain

whether the business is built on a foundation that provides relevant, client focused services/products and availability of a market that will pay a fair price to enable the organization to sustain its activities over the medium term at least. There should be certainty about the assumptions upon which the business model is based and whether they have been tested on a regular basis to ensure viability that can be maintained. The board should continually challenge itself on these most important matters.

3. **Stakeholder Engagement:** The organization in general and the board in particular, should understand who the key stakeholders are, how they interact with the business and how they are engaged to ensure the best outcome for the organization. The organization should ascertain whether stakeholder engagement has been included in the annual agenda and strategic plan.

4. **Risk Management:** The organization should have a risk management plan in place, and is to be reviewed over the year and updated on an annual basis. The board should make a discussion each year on its appetite for risk, and how it impacts on its risk management plan and how the risk will be managed during the year. There should be a business continuity plan in place.

5. **Performance Management:** It is about the way the organization, the CEO and the board handles the management of performance for each plan. Every board member should have a real understanding of how the organization is performing both historically and in terms of lead indicators. The board should have a system in place to monitor the performance of the CEO and an opportunity to provide mutual feedback on an annual basis. The board should review its own performance and seek ways to enhance its own functioning.

6. **Compliance:** This pertains to the organization having a culture of compliance that "it is the right thing to do rather than something that must be done to avoid penalties." It is a register in place to assist in compliance management and to provide evidence to the board of how this is being managed within the organization.

7. **Professional Development & Succession:** These are resources allocated for ongoing professional development of the board and be certain that there is an annual plan in place that demonstrates this has been thought about within the context of the board's needs. It is also about whether there is a plan in place for board renewal that both retains knowledge and experience and ensures appropriate representation.

4.8. Good Governance in National Government

Good governance in the context of countries is a broad term, and in that regards, it is difficult to find a unique definition. According to Fukuyama (2013),[45] there are two dimensions to qualify governance as good or bad: the capacity of the state and the bureaucracy's autonomy. They both complement, in the sense that when the state is more capable, for instance through the collection of taxes, there should be more autonomy because the bureaucrats are able to conduct things well without being instructed with a lot of details. In less capable states, however, less discretion and more rules setting are desirable.

Another way to think about good governance is through outcomes. Since governments carry out with goals like the provision of public goods to its citizens, there is no better way to think about good governance other than through deliverables, which are precisely the one demanded by citizens, like security, health,

---

45   Fukuyama, Francis (January 2013). "What Is Governance?". Center for Global Development. Working paper 314.

education, water, the enforcement of contracts, protection to property, protection to the environment and their ability to vote and get paid fair wages.[46]

Similarly, good governance might be approximated with provision of public services in an efficient manner, higher participation given to certain groups in the population like the poor and the minorities, the guarantee that citizens have the opportunity of checks and balances on the government, the establishment and enforcement of norms for the protection of the citizens and their property and the existence of independent judiciary systems.[47]

Lawson (2011)[48] in his review of Rothstein's book *The quality of government: corruption, social trust, and inequality in international perspective* [49]mentions that the author relates good governance to the concept of impartiality, which is basically when the bureaucrats perform their tasks following the public interest rather than their self-interest. Lawson differs with him in that this impartial application of law ignores important factors like the economic liberalism, which matters due to its relation with economic growth.

4.9. Good Governance in Local Government

Good governance is argued to be the most important aspect in local governments. It tries to promote more relationships between government and:

---

46   Rotberg, Robert (July 2014). "Good Governance Means Performance and Results". Governance. 27 (3): 511–518. doi:10.1111/gove.12084

47   Grindle, Merilee (October 2004). "Good Enough Governance: Poverty Reduction and Reform in Developing Countries". Governance. 17 (4): 525–48. doi:10.1111/j.0952-1895.2004.00256.x

48   Lawson, Robert (2012). "Book Review of Bo Rothstein: The quality of government: corruption, social trust, and inequality in international perspective". Public Choice. 150(3–4): 793–795. doi:10.1007/s11127-011-9903-y.

49   Fukuyama, Francis (January 2013). "What Is Governance?". Center for Global Development. Working paper 314.

1. Empowered citizens.
2. Neighborhood councils.
3. Community councils.

Good governance with local government aims to increase civil engagement with more members of the community in order to get the best options that serves the people.[50]

Local governance is made up of the political and institutional processes through which decisions are taken and implemented. Local governance is most effective when these processes are participatory, accountable, transparent, efficient, inclusive, and respect the rule of law.

4.10. Different Perspectives about Good Governance
4.10.1. United Nations

The United Nations (UN) is playing an increasing role in good governance. According to former UN Secretary-General Kofi Annan, "Good governance is ensuring respect for human rights and the rule of law; strengthening democracy; promoting transparency and capacity in public administration." To implement this, the UN follows eight principles:[51]

1. **Participation**–People should be able to voice their own opinions through legitimate immediate organizations or representatives.

2. **Rule of Law**–Legal framework should be enforced impartially, especially on human right laws.

3. **Consensus Oriented**–Mediates differing interests to meet the broad consensus on the best interests of a community.

---

50   "A User's Guide to Measuring Local Governance" UNDP.
51   "What is Good Governance". UNESCAP, 2009. Accessed April 6, 2021.

4. **Equity and Inclusiveness**–People should have opportunities to improve or maintain their well-being.

5. **Effectiveness and Efficiency**–Processes and institutions should be able to produce results that meet the needs of their community while making the best of their resources.

6. **Accountability**–Governmental institutions, private sectors, and civil society organizations should be held accountable to the public and institutional stakeholders.

7. **Transparency**–Information should be accessible to the public and should be understandable and monitored.

8. **Responsiveness**–Institutions and processes should serve all stakeholders.

4.10.2. International Monetary Fund

The International Monetary Fund (IMF) was created at a United Nations (UN) conference in Bretton Woods, New Hampshire. In 1996, the IMF declared promoting good governance in all its aspects, including by ensuring the rule of law, improving the efficiency and accountability of the public sector, and tackling corruption, as essential elements of a framework within which economies can prosper.[52]

The IMF feels that corruption within economies is caused by the ineffective governance of the economy, either too much regulation or too little regulation.[53] To receive loans from the IMF, countries must have certain good governance policies, as determined by the IMF, in place.[54]

---

52   "The IMF's Approach to Promoting Good Governance and Combating Corruption — A Guide". International Monetary Fund. June 20, 2005. Retrieved November 2, 2009.
53   Ibid.
54   Ibid.

4.10.3. World Bank

The World Bank introduced the concept in its 1992 report entitled "Governance and Development". According to the document, good governance is an essential complement to sound economic policies and is central to creating and sustaining an environment which fosters strong and equitable development. For the World Bank, good governance consists of components which are: capacity and efficiency in public sector management, accountability, legal framework for development, and information and transparency.[55]

The Worldwide Governance Indicators is a program funded by the World Bank to measure the quality of governance of over 200 countries. It uses six dimensions of governance for their measurements, Voice & Accountability, Political Stability and Lack of Violence, Government Effectiveness, Regulatory Quality, Rule of Law, and Control of Corruption. They have been studying countries since 1996.[56]

4.10.4. International Humanitarian Funding

Good governance defines an ideal that is difficult to achieve in full, though it is something development supporters consider donating to causes.[57] Major donors and international financial institutions, like the International Monetary Fund (IMF) or World Bank, are basing their aid and loans on the condition that the recipient undertake reforms ensuring good governance.[58] This is mostly due to the close link between poor governance and corruption.[59]

---

55   http://documents.worldbank.org/curated/en/604951468739447676/pdf/multi-page.pdf.

56   Kaufmann, Daniel and Kraay, Aart, "Growth Without Governance" (November 2002). World Bank Policy Research Working Paper No. 2928.

57   Op. Cit. Agere. P. 2.

58   "What is Good Governance". UNESCAP, 2009. Accessed April 6, 2021.

59   "The IMF and Good Governance", IMF. Accessed August 12, 2009.

4.10.5. Democratization

Because concepts such as civil society, decentralization, peaceful conflict management and accountability are often used when defining the concept of good governance, the definition of good governance promotes many ideas that closely align with effective democratic governance.[60]

Not surprisingly, emphasis on good governance can sometimes be equated with promoting democratic government. However, a 2011 literature review analyzing the link between democracy and development by Alina Rocha Menocal of the Overseas Development Institute stresses the inconclusiveness of evidence on this relationship. [61]

A good example of this close association, for some actors, between western democratic governance and the concept of good governance is the following statement made by U.S. Secretary of State Hillary Clinton in Nigeria on August 12, 2009:

Again, to refer to President Obama's speech, what Africa needs is not more strong men; it needs more strong democratic institutions that will stand the test of time. Without good governance, no amount of oil or no amount of aid, no amount of effort can guarantee Nigeria's success. But with good governance, nothing can stop Nigeria. It's the same message that I have carried in all of my meetings, including my meeting this afternoon with your president. The United States supports the seven-point agenda for reform that was outlined by President Yar'Adua. We believe that delivering on roads and on electricity and on education and all the other points of that agenda will demonstrate the kind of concrete progress that the people of Nigeria are waiting for.

---

60   Op. Cit. Agere. P. 10.
61   Rocha Menocal, A. (2011) "Analyzing the relationship between democracy and development", Overseas Development Institute.

4.10.6. Role of Political Parties

Researchers at the Overseas Development Institute have criticized past studies of good governance to place too little importance on developing political parties, their capacity and their ties to their grassroots supporters. [62]

While political parties play a key role in well-functioning democracies, elsewhere political parties are disconnected from voters and dominated by elites, with few incentives or capabilities to increase the representation of other voters. [63]

Political parties can play a key role in pivotal moments of a state's development, either negatively (e.g. organizing and instigating violence) or positively (e.g. by leading dialogue in a fractured society). [64]

While differences in the electoral system play their role in defining the number of parties and their influence once in power (proportional, first past the post, etc.), the funding and expertise available to parties also plays an important role not only in their existence, but their ability to connect to a broad base of support. [65]

While the United Nations Development Program and the European Commission have been providing funds to political parties since the 1990s, there are still calls to increase the support for capacity development activities including the development of party manifestos, party constitutions and campaigning skills.[66]

---

62   Foresti and Wild 2010. "Support to political parties: a missing piece of the governance puzzle". London: Overseas Development Institute.
63   Ibid.
64   Ibid.
65   Ibid.
66   Ibid.

4.10.7. Scholarly Approaches

Nayef Al-Rodhan, in his 2009 book *Sustainable History and the Dignity of Man: A Philosophy of History and Civilisational Triumph*, proposed eight minimum criteria for ensuring good national governance. [67] Al-Rodhan's eight minimum criteria are:

1. Participation, equity, and inclusiveness;
2. Rule of law;
3. Separation of powers;
4. Free, independent, and responsible media;
5. Government legitimacy;
6. Accountability;
7. Transparency; and
8. Limiting the distorting effect of money in politics.

In the book, he argues that good national governance is an important component in creating a history of sustainability for the human race. For Al-Rodhan, the eight minimal criteria of good governance are expressions of the fundamental values of democracy and more liberal constitutionalism.

The Tuskegee Study from 1932 to 1972 led to the signing of the National Research Act. This law outlined basic ethical ways in which research is to be carried out. The Department of Health, Education, and Welfare (DHEW) made regulations that required voluntary agreements for anyone who was to take part in their studies. Governance is used in scientific studies to ensure that policies are safe and ethical when studies are being done on human subjects. After the National Research Act there had been other organization put in place such as the Ethics Advisory Board, which reviews

---

67   Al-Rodhan, Nayef R. F., Sustainable History and the Dignity of Man: A Philosophy of History and Civilisational Triumph, LIT, 2009.

biomedical research. Many federal agencies adopted the Federal Policy for Protection of Human Rights in 1991. In 1995 President Bill Clinton established the National Bioethics Advisory Commission led by the Department of Health and Human Services with the task of reviewing regulations and policies to ensure the safety of research volunteers.[68]

4.11. Criticisms

According to Sam Agere, "The discretionary space left by the lack of a clear well-defined scope for what governance encompasses allows users to choose and set their own parameters."[69]

In the book *Contesting 'good' governance*, Eva Poluha and Mona Rosendahl contested standards that are common to western democracy as measures of "goodness" in government.[70] By applying political anthropological methods, they concluded that while governments believe they apply concepts of good governance while making decisions, cultural differences can cause conflict with the heterogeneous standards of the international community.[71]

An additional source of good governance criticism is *The Intelligent Person's Guide to Good Governance*, written by Surendra Munshi. Munshi's work was created in order to "revive" good governance. Many individuals tend to either wave away and are bored with the idea of governance, or not have a clue to

---

68   "How Tuskegee Changed Research Practices". Center for Disease Control and Prevention, April 4, 2016.
69   Cit. Agere. P.4.
70   Poluha, Eva; Rosendahl, Mona (2002). Contesting 'good' governance:crosscultural perspectives on representation, accountability and public space. Routledge. ISBN 978-0-7007-1494-0
71   Poluha, Eva; Rosendahl, Mona (2002). Contesting 'good' governance:crosscultural perspectives on representation, accountability and public space. Routledge. ISBN 978-0-7007-1494-0

what it has at all. This book is a generalized discussion on what the purpose of good governance is and how it serves that purpose throughout our society. Munshi targets the book toward anyone doing research or just simply "those concerned with the issue of governance."[72]

Rethinking Systems: Configurations of Politics and Policy in Contemporary Governance, written by Michael P. Crozier, is another work analyzing good governance. Crozier's article discusses the different dynamics of changes that occur throughout communication systems and the effect it has on governance.[73]

The idea of various perspectives is presented throughout the article. This allows the reader to be able to see what contemporary governance is like from different viewpoints. Crozier's motive was to also create an open mindset when referring to how governance and policy within society operate, especially with the constant changes occurring day to day.

4.12. Reformation of Good Governance

Three institutions can be reformed to promote good governance: the state, the private sector and civil society. However, among different cultures, the need and demand for reform can vary depending on the priorities of that country's society. A variety of country level initiatives and international movements put emphasis on various types of governance reform. Each movement

---

72   Munshi, Surendra; Abraham, Biju Paul; Chaudhuri, Soma (March 12, 2009). The intelligent person's guide to good governance. New Delhi, India: Sage Publications. ISBN 9788178299310.
73   Crozier, Michael P. (July 16, 2010). "Rethinking Systems". Administration & Society. 42 (5): 504–525. doi:10.1177/0095399710377443.

for reform establishes criteria for what they consider good governance based on their own needs and agendas.[74]

---

74   Internet.

CHAPTER FIVE

LOCAL GOVERNMENT ADMINISTRATION IN SOUTH SUDAN

5.1. Introduction

South Sudan is part and parcel of the Sudan since the creation of the modern Sudanese state in the 19ᵗʰ century. Subsequently, any historical background of any matter about South Sudan has to refer to the old practice in the Sudan.

The Turkish rule in the Sudan from 1821 until the Mahdist regime, the system of government in the Sudan was centralized one. The same with the Condominium rule which adopted the kind of rule which they called "Direct Rule" from 1898 to 1924. It was a period of pacification and maintenance of law and order.

The establishment of local government institutions in southern Sudan is traced back to time immemorial. In 1921, the then Government of the Sudan declared a policy based on the principle of decentralization. It was based on the recommendation made in

1920 that Sudan has a vast land and heterogeneous population and it would have been reasonable to leave the administration of remote areas in the Sudan to the native authorities under the supervision of British Administrators.

The decentralization system was declared with the principle to make use of indigenous agents where applicable and to take charge of a few administrative responsibilities. In the process of its development, it was envisaged to subsequently result into economic viability and rise of administrative standard.

5.2. The Origin of Local Government Administration in South Sudan

5.2.1. Indirect Rule

Local government of the Sudan grew out "of what is variously called Indirect Rule or Native Administration." [75]

Indirect Rule means in colonial parlance ruling through native agencies, usually chiefs, emirs, and nazirs.[76] Until 1937 the system that was followed was that of "the conventional successful colonial policy of using native courts and native authorities, of entrusting them with local powers of administration, justice and finance."[77]

It was in the northern Sudan that "native administration legislation ran through a series of ordinances such as 'Powers of Nomad Sheikhs, Powers of Sheikhs, Native Courts' 1922-30". Afterwards the "Title Local Government replaced Native Administration which had become a slogan, a Delphic Oracle to some political officers, and anathema to some departmental officials and urban effendia."[78]

---

75   Henderson, K. D. D., The Making of the Modern Sudan, Faber and Faber Limited, London, UK, 1953. P. 531.
76   Ibid. P. 532.
77   Ibid. P. 532.
78   Ibid. P. 532.

Southern Sudan was excluded from these ordinances because "…southern provinces' conditions differ widely from those prevalent in the northern and central area of the Sudan. To McMichael and his generation in the central government, that difference was an unbridgeable gap: the south was an area of speculation, no more comprehensible than the human mind, mysterious, unknown, and better left that way."[79]

However, "In accordance with the spirit of The Powers of Nomad Sheikhs Ordinance, which was not applied in the south, the government also resolved to 'leave administration, as far as possible, in the hands of native authorities, wherever they exist'; where 'local or tribal organization' had 'ceased to exist', it might 'still be possible to re-create it'. There was no urgency in these decisions, hedged as they were with qualifications and unaccompanied by suggestions for their implementation. Moreover, the expressed resolved to rule through 'native chiefs' was even less appropriate in the south, with its acephalous peoples, than in the north."[80]

From 1924 to 1932 Indirect Rule was applied in the Sudan. "Native Courts Ordinances of 1931 and 1932, the system of native administration throughout the whole country took permanent shape. More administrative and then financial powers were devolved to the new tribal administrations. However native administration proved to be, in the late 1930s, a rigid system of administration favoring only the unchanging conditions of medieval tribal life."[81]

The principle of native administration was that a European Administrator was incapable of imparting administration among the

---

79   Daly, M. W. Empire on The Nile: The Anglo-Egyptian Sudan 1898-1934. Cambridge University Press, Great Britain, 1986. P. 396.

80   Ibid. P. 405.

81   Galobawi Mohamed Salih. The Heritage of Local Government. In: John Howell (ed.) Local Government and Politics in the Sudan. Khartoum, Sudan, Khartoum University Press, 1974. P. 23.

natives. The Central Government was to create a conducive atmosphere to maintain law and order and no interference in tribal organizations activities or functions. The tribal administration, for example, had neither the desire nor capability to provide urgently needed public services such as education, sanitation and public works.[82]

Indirect rule was based on The Lugardian Theory "the cardinal principal upon which the administration of almost every British dependency in Africa was based between the two world wars, never succeeded in gaining a firm footing in the Sudan. However the potential value of certain features of it fascinated the minds of Khartoum officers and their colleagues in the provincial capitals. Thus by the time 'classical' indirect rule had been established in Northern Nigeria (with attempts to rule the native population through their own institutions and conferring on native traditional executives real and defined powers), Sudan British administrators were taking the lead in the direction of another 'revisionist' indirect rule policy. They had been instructed by Lord Kitchener to base their authority on the confidence of the people and to attain that confidence through personal contacts and private dealings with the members of the higher class of natives (who would in turn influence the masses under their control). And thus field officers in the Sudan came to interpret indirect rule differently from their colleagues elsewhere in Africa."[83]

Indirect rule was a kind of 'a Pragmatic Approach'. It meant to be "a discretionary attitude, uncast in any mould that would enable individual officers to achieve their ends by persuasion, moral or otherwise, through the use of intermediaries. They had no place in

82   Ibid. P. 23.
83   Gaafar Mohamed Ali Bakheit. The Condominium and Indirect Rule .In: John Howell (ed.). Local Government and Politics in the Sudan, Khartoum, Sudan, Khartoum Printing Press, 1974. P. 25.

their designs for Lugard-type native chiefs who were an 'integral part of the machinery of Government with well defined powers and functions recognized by Government and by law.' In the choice and employment of native agents the British administration in the Sudan refused to commit itself to any one agency, policy or class of natives and preferred a game in which players changed places and were interchangeable themselves. Statutory provisions were slow to emerge, and were often regarded as necessary evils, as they tied the hands of the Government whose members were worried by the tendency of institutional organization to freeze relations between the alien ruler and the native agent in formal patterns, thereby stultifying their development.[84]

The two main virtues of indirect rule were its role as an expediency in overcoming the dearth of men and money while building up administrative organs that would provide relative security; and its effect as a principle of government in preserving the indigenous cultural values of local communities and protecting their identities from being eroded by subversive elements. Neither of these virtues impressed the Sudan Government staff. Thus strengths of indirect rule, firstly as an inexpensive executive agency and secondly as a cultural fortress, were not easily accepted in the Sudan.[85]

The justifications put forward by Lugard in support of his choice of indirect rule "had little significance in the Sudan since the hierarchy of *mudirs*, inspectors and *mamurs* assisted by *muawins* and police officers could already provide a core of central authority in every district of the Sudan. Executive authority was expanding, measures for economic development were in hand, educational institutions were already in operation and the agents for a direct form of rule were chosen from the new generation and not the old one. Plans

---

84   Ibid. P. 25.
85   Ibid. P. 26.

for making use of tribal elements in the administrative, judicial and financial spheres of the administration had been devised consciously as issues of policies directed towards a set of goal and guided by well-defined motives as early 1916-1917. But it was not the intention of the Government to accord these tribal elements a separate identity but to use them politically as a lever against the religious sectarian forces and as a pretext to get rid of Egyptian monopoly of field administration. It was also a justification for increasing the number of British staff and extending their authority into-day-to-day affairs. Absurd as it might look; British officers used tribal agents in order to get more British officers to supervise them and called for decentralization only in order to achieve Deconcentration, which in effect was simply a devise for centralization. Distrustful of the innate qualities of the indigenous communities they governed, the British administrators did not believe in the wisdom of leaving people to themselves to manage their affairs according to tribal custom and usage, and subject to very limited restrictions."[86]

Indirect rule as a principle meant a conservative philosophy that sustained the preservation of indigenous political institutions intact, to serve as a bases for future development, and as a means of adopting what could be adapted to local needs, of civilized norms, practices and institutions. As a method of administration the system of indirect rule had been developed to consist of a native authority, normally single and autocratic, that was part of machinery of government with defined powers of judicial, fiscal and executive nature which were exercised under statutory authority. Powers varied in degree according to the stage of development reached by the authority concerned. In the exercise of their powers native authorities were subject to the direction of the administrative

---

86   Ibid. PP. 26-27.

officers who acted as appealate, revising authorities. Finally, each authority administered its own treasury fed by revenue from local taxes. The emphasis of the system was on the preservation of 'rule' and upholding the authority of chiefs.[87]

Of course the theory of indirect rule even in Northern Nigeria itself did not remain as a specific dogma for which there was only one aspect in application. Handled by men of varied temperaments, it developed into a tradition comprising different schools of thought and describing policies of such diverse countries as Biafra and Zandeland. The principle of indirect rule had continually to be defined and restated; in the process, the vague tradition went out of fashion and 'Native Administration' gained currency as both a replacement and development of 'Indirect Rule.'[88]

5.2.2 Native Administration

Native administration, on the other hand, emerged from another indirect rule school and that is local government administration associated with the name of Sir Donald Cameron. To Cameron a local authority meant more than an autocratic chief. It covered chiefs, chiefs in councils, councils of chiefs and non-chiefs. The emphasis of the system was shifted from the preservation of chieftainships and stereotyping their institutions, to the evolution towards representative local government. Native authorities were to be gradually but persistently transferred into institutions, deriving their legitimacy, not from any inherited right, but from being acceptable to the people. Cameron indicated that the essence of indirect administration was the administration of Africans as far as possible through the instrument of their own indigenous institutions. He emphasized the necessity of ascertaining whether the indigenous institutions

---

87   Ibid. P. 27.
88   Ibid. P. 27.

acting as native authorities were really authoritative and whether or not they were able to shoulder new responsibilities in the service of the people. He described the system as the recognition of native authorities as self-governing local executives, with clearly defined responsibilities, judicial, legislative and executive, enjoying under supervision, and their own sources of revenue and a definite sphere of expenditure. In Cameron's perception, native authorities have to be local executives, with the implication that whenever they proved their worth, they would be allowed some latitude of autonomy in discharging their responsibilities.[89]

The step which Cameron had taken in emphasizing the role of native administration had led native authorities to work more and more as central government agencies for the provision of services, thus assuming responsibilities for which they were not fitted traditionally, and thus gaining financial resources far beyond their limited means of customary dues and gifts. There was thus an evolution towards something resembling a 'modern' local government system in which local bodies, elected or not, exercised powers devolved upon them by the central government.[90]

5.2.3. Local Government

The Sudan was ahead of many African countries when in 1934 the Governor-General, Sir George Stewart Symes, adopted the policy of confining native agencies to areas that were predominantly tribal and could not in the near future develop economically or socially. Instead of 'Native Administration', Symes said there should be 'local government' geared to keep public security and order, to provide social services, to train Sudanese in the art of government, to absorb nationalist sentiment and to divert enthusiastic patriotism into the

---

89   Ibid. P. 28.
90   Ibid. P. 30.

service of concrete constructive ends. The tribal native authority in the Cameron style was to become a local government authority until the time was opportune to democratize the system. The Local Government Ordinances of 1937 for the Rural Areas, Townships and Municipalities and their 1938 Regulations, indicate the role which the Sudan Government had envisaged for native administration. It was to be developed so as to be absorbed into a system of 'democratic' local government.[91]

It was in 1936/37 that the system of local government started. In 1936, the British began to adapt 'native administration' into 'local government'-an administration no longer according to the tribe a man belonged to, but according to the place he lived. A series of ordinances in 1937 enacted modernized principles of local self-government, providing for parallel organizations, differing in only degree, for municipalities, townships and rural areas. The importance of the Rural District Councils was that they were a step towards detribalization, providing a democratic and territorial framework through which the tribal leaders would function in association with other representative elements, instead of continuing to exercise separate and individual powers. The system of local government was based primarily on the English practice.[92]

It was until 1942 that Provincial Advisory Councils were created to advise the Provincial Governor. These councils were not independent in terms of budgets or buildings for running their affairs. There were no cadres of officers trained especially to run the instituted system of local government. As such, rural councils were mainly run by Chiefs who were acting like Kings. The towns were run by *Mamurs*.

The real system of local government got established in the Sudan as a result of Dr. Arthur Hedley Marshal report in 1949. After Dr.

---

91   Ibid. P. 30.
92   Op. Cit. Galobawi. P. 23.

Marshal's report was exhaustively examined by province and local councils, Local Government Advisory Board and finally by the Executive Council and Legislative Assembly, the Report's recommendations were implemented in Local Government Ordinance 1951 which repealed and superseded the former laws.[93]

Local Government Councils were created by separate warrants, or charters, issued by the central government,[94] and they became to have independent budgets. Separate personnel officers were trained to run the Local Government Administration and to be in charge of running services. Any understanding of local government in the Sudan today must start with an examination of the system which evolved from the 1951 Ordinance.[95]

In May 1954, a Ministry of Local Government was created to act as a clearing house for the central government for local affairs. The Ministry was given the task of coordinating the work of all central departments' field administrations and of acting as the representative of the national government for the development and supervision of local government authorities in the country at large... By the end of 1950s, warrants had been issued to over sixty local government councils in the Sudan. Under these, the local council was recognized as a corporate body of perpetual existence, with its own financial resources, and power to maintain its own staff, to provide important local services, to make and execute policy, and to pass laws of local application.[96]

An important modification to the structure of local government came with the Provincial Administration Act of 1960. The Act was based on

---

93   Ibid. P. 24.
94   Galobawi Mohamed Salih. Local Government after Independence. In: John Howell (ed.), Local Government and Politics in the Sudan. Khartoum, Sudan, Khartoum University Press, !974. P.33.
95   Ibid. P. 33.
96   Ibid. P. 33.

the Report of the Commission on Coordination between Central and Local Government or the Abu Rannat Commission Report.

The office of the District Commissioner was abolished by the Provincial Administration Act 1960.[97] The Act was based on the Report of the Commission on Coordination between Central and Local Government or the Abu Rannat Commission Report.[98] The Provincial Councils were created as policy-making body within the province. It was intended to improve on coordination between the centre and the provinces. It had two tier systems: the council was a policy-making body chaired by the Military Governor with its secretary as the Civilian Governor and members drawn from the districts through co-option.

The Province Executive Authority was also created as an implementation body of the resolutions passed by the Province Council. The Provincial Executive Authority was headed by the Civilian Governor who was the secretary of the Province Executive Authority. The 1960 Act was criticized as a move toward central-ization and an administrative strategy for popularization of military policies. The Act became ineffective. This system got abolished at the end of 1964 and return to the system of 1951 Local Government Ordinance.

During the May Revolution of 1969 era, the system of local government was reviewed and the outcome was the People's Local Government Act 1971. "It involves, primarily, a large measure of administrative and executive decentralization away from the capital, Khartoum, to what in 1973 were the ten provinces of Darfur, Kordofan, Northern, Blue Nile, Kassala, Red Sea, Khartoum, Equatoria, Bahr el Ghazal and Upper Nile. This acquisition of new powers by the provinces has been paralled by a diminution of the

---

97   Ibid. P. 33.
98   Ibid. P. 43.

powers of the old council authorities."[99]

The objective of 1971 Act was that all administrative units and political organizations were to be mobilized in support of the May Revolution. There was no political neutrality. The whole society was to be revolutionized and attitudes changed.

The main feature of 1971 Act was creation of two administrative organs: the Provincial Executive Council (PEC) and the Provincial Commissioner (PC). The PEC was a corporate body with delegated authority in so many areas, including political participation and building organs of the Sudanese Socialist Union (SSU). The Province Commissioner was the representative of the government at the provincial level exercising both the political and the executive authority. The commissioner was to be an efficient administrator, skilled and politically conscious person and ardent supporter of the May Revolution. He was appointed by the President of the Republic of the Sudan. The Commissioner was the Chairman of the Province Executive council and the representative of the President in the province. He was the Chief Security Officer of the province and in this respect he writes security reports to the Minister of Interior. The Commissioner was also the treasurer of the Province Executive Council. He makes decisions in the absence of the Province Executive Council. He has powers to suspend the resolutions of the Province Executive Council. The system was centralization at the provincial level although there existed councils at the levels of the town, rural, quarter, market, industrial, village or nomadic camps.

Under Self-Government Act, 1972 Southern Sudan became autonomous region with three provinces of Bahr el Ghazal,

---

99   John Howell. The Reform of Local Government, 1971. In: John Howell (ed.) Local Government and Politics in the Sudan. Khartoum, Sudan, Khartoum University, 1974. P. 65.

Equatoria and Upper Nile. Later on Lakes, Jonglei and Western Equatoria Provinces were created. These provinces were administered by commissioners under the People's Local Government Act, 1971.[100]

In 1980, the People's Province Executive Councils under 1971 Act were revised and in 1981 it was replaced with the People's Local Government Act 1981, which created twenty five Area Councils for the Southern Sudan. Area Councils were independent corporate bodies which had their own budgets. They were entrusted powers to generate revenues from local resources and receive subsidy from the central government.[101]

In 1983, Southern Sudan was divided into three regions of Equatoria, Bahr el Ghazal and Upper Nile and each region was administered by an independent regional governor. Consequently, the previous provincial towns of Juba, Malakal and Wau were upgraded to the status of regional capitals. A number of new provinces were created in the three Southern Regions, for example, Raja in Bahr el Ghazal region was created as a reward for supporting division of the South.[102]

The system of 1971 Act was criticized because it made the Commissioner to be autocratic or as feudal lord/king within the province because of the misuse of powers. Because of the criticism of the 1971 Act, it was replaced by 1981 People's Local Government Act. Some of the weaknesses in 1971 Act were modified. The province was not any longer the unit of local government administration. The territories of the province were very large and the local government system was not effective in rendering services. The

---

100   Dhal, A. Matoc, Local Government Financing in Southern Sudan, Khartoum University Press, Khartoum, Sudan, 2002. P. 13.
101   Ibid. P. 13.
102   Ibid. P. 13.

provincial boundaries in the 1971 Act were like regional boundaries in 1981 Act. The People's Local Government Act 1981 created area councils which were like district councils. The area councils were corporate bodies and legal entities within the Local government system.

The office of the commissioner was retained but its jurisdiction was limited to specific functions which were mainly maintenance of security within the province, the supervision of police, prisons and fire brigade forces, the maintenance of the secondment system between the personnel requirements of the area councils and the regional governments, supervision and inspection of area councils, rendering reports on the activities of the area councils to the Governor of the Region, and any other functions that may be delegated to him from time to time.

When war broke out in the Sudan from 16th May 1983, South Sudan became divided into towns under the Government of the Sudan or the three Regions of southern Sudan by then and administration was generally paralyzed in southern Sudan. Local government administration in southern Sudan was particularly affected and no services were being rendered to the citizens. Areas that were captured by the Sudan People's Liberation Army/Movement (SPLA/M) in the country were declared by the leadership of the SPLA/M as New Sudan. Other Local Government Acts promulgated by Sudan Government during the war period, from 1983 up to 2005 were never effected in southern Sudan due to the raging war at that time.

From 1984 the SPLA/M had no act or law regulating Local Government Administration in the New Sudan. New Sudan was divided into Zones under the rule of Military Officers.

It was until 1991 that SPLA/M held a meeting in Torit and

came out with a resolution diving powers between Civil Military Officers (CMOs) and Civil Military Administrators (CMAs). Torit Resolution of 1991 allowed appointment of Commanders to be heads of the Zones. This stage can be considered as the foundation for formation of local authority that was made of Civil Military Officers and Civil Military Administrators. The law practiced at that time was military law.

In 1994 the Chukudum Convention was convened. The Chukudum Convention resolved the appointment of separate civil administrators from the military officers. The structure adopted by the Chukudum Convention was as in the figure 5.1. It was a kind of federal system where the Governors report to the Chairman of the Sudan People's Liberation Movement and Commander in Chief of the SPLA. The Governors were the heads of the governments at the Regional level. The regions were Bahr el Ghazal, Equatoria, Ingasana (in eastern Blue Nile), Nuba Mountains (in Southern Kordofan) and Upper Nile.

A chart was drawn to illustrate the different positions of local and national governments. The chart was intended to show the physical and the functional relationships between the various structural levels of government within the national government system. Here below the by then New Sudan Structure of the Federal Government and Local government Administration.

Figure 5.1 Shows the Structure
of Government of the New Sudan

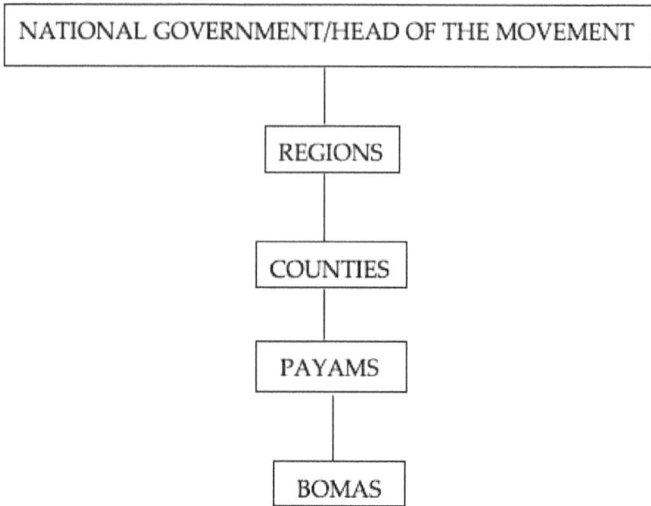

```
┌─────────────────────────────────────────────────┐
│  NATIONAL GOVERNMENT/HEAD OF THE MOVEMENT         │
└─────────────────────────────────────────────────┘
                        │
                ┌───────────────┐
                │    REGIONS     │
                └───────────────┘
                        │
                ┌───────────────┐
                │   COUNTIES     │
                └───────────────┘
                        │
                ┌───────────────┐
                │    PAYAMS      │
                └───────────────┘
                        │
                ┌───────────────┐
                │     BOMAS      │
                └───────────────┘
```

This structure was embodied in the Comprehensive Peace Agreement (CPA) of 2005 between the Government of Sudan under the leadership of President Omer Ahmed Al Bashier and Sudan People's Liberation Movement/Army under the leadership of Dr. John Garang de Mabior. Therefore this structure was adapted as structure of governance for Government of Southern Sudan (GoSS), and as well for the Republic of South Sudan (RSS).

Decentralization was embodied in the CPA and later enshrined in both the Interim Constitution of the Sudan, 2005 and the Interim Constitution of Southern Sudan, 2005. The CPA gave powers to Southern Sudan Government (GoSS) to promulgate its own laws and subsequently in 2009; Local Government Act was passed by the Legislative Assembly of Southern Sudan and became the law for governing Local Government Administration in Southern Sudan up to this date.

5.3. Objectives for the Creation of Regions, Counties, Payams and Bomas in the New Sudan

There was nowhere has the objectives for creation of what is considered as local government administration in the New Sudan been spelled out. It is from the key categories of civil county administrators work were it could be deduced that the objectives for creation of local government administration in the New Sudan were framed as follows:

a. **Administration of law and order:** This included provision of good governance, insure delivery of justice, protection of rights and freedom and promotion of community initiatives.

b. **Social Services to the Community:** Includes promotion of the development of basic services, train and enlighten communities on development and promote rural development.

c. **Managing Resources:** Dealing with over grazing issues, mobilize human and material resources for development, sensitizing communities on proper use of resources for development, plan development programs, provide control and organize people affairs.

d. **Responding to Relief and Emergency Needs:** Assist returnees and other emergency relief actions, responding to outbreak of animal diseases.

e. **Cultural Development:** Respect cultures and traditions and their development, and promotion of social cultural activities.

f. **Representation and Policy:** Forwarding community issues to higher authorities, promotion of cooperation among the communities, coordinate policy development; disseminate policies of civil administration among the communities and promotion of unity among the tribes.

5.4. The Authority of Local Government in South Sudan

Local government authority in South Sudan is derived from the people and is exercised in accordance with the people's will as prescribed in Local Government Act, 2009, and any other applicable laws. The authority is vested in each council which is a legal entity with the right to sue and be sued in its own name. The authority in each Local Government Council is exercised through the democratic and representative institutions of government established in accordance with the provisions of Local Government Act, 2009.

5.5. Objectives of Local Government in South Sudan

The objectives of local government in South Sudan are as hereunder (LGA, 2009):

1. To promote self governance and enhance the participation of people and communities in maintaining law and order and promoting democratic, transparent and accountable local government;
2. To establish the local government institutions as close as possible to the people;
3. To encourage the involvement of communities and community based organizations in local governance and promote dialogue among them on matters of local interest;
4. To promote and facilitate civic education;
5. To promote social and economic development;
6. To promote self-reliance amongst the people through mobilization of local resources to ensure the provision of services to communities in a sustainable manner;
7. To promote peace, reconciliation and peaceful co-existence among the various communities;

8. To ensure gender mainstreaming in local government;
9. To acknowledge and incorporate the role of traditional authorities and customary law in the local government system;
10. To consult and involve communities in decision making relating to the exploitation of natural resources in their areas;
11. To create and promote safe and healthy environment; and
12. To encourage and support women and youth activities and the training of local cadres.

5.6. Principles of Local Government in South Sudan

The principles of local government in South Sudan are as the following (LGA, 2009):

1. The principle of subsidiarity, where decisions and functions are delegated to the lowest competent level of government;
2. Self governance and democracy;
3. Participation of all citizens in the exercise of their rights to express their opinions in the process of decision making in public affairs;
4. Rule of law, maintain law and order and its enforcement in a fair and impartial manner while respecting and honouring the norms, virtues and values of the society;
5. Transparency, to build mutual trust between government and citizens through the provision of information and guaranteed access to information;
6. Equity, to provide equal services and opportunities for all members of the local community with the aim of improving their welfare; responsiveness, to increase the sensitivity of the employees of government and non-governmental organizations to the aspirations of the people in service delivery and meeting public demands;

7. Accountability, to ensure accountability of decision makers to the people in all matters of public interest; and

8. Efficiency and effectiveness, to ensure good public service delivery through optimum and responsible use of resources.

5.7. Tiers of Local Government in South Sudan

Local government in South Sudan is a decentralized system of administrative tiers and has a devolved authority and into which the Traditional Authority is incorporated. The tiers of Local government are as follows (LGA, 2009):

1. The County, City, Municipal and Town Councils;

2. The Payam and Block Councils which are Coordinative Administrative Units; and

3. The Boma and Quarter Councils which are Basic Administrative Units.

The names of the Counties and number of the Payams and Bomas which were created before the independence of South Sudan-time of CANS are as in Appendix I. Table 5.1 shows the summary of the Counties, Payams and Bomas of the ten States.

Table 5.1 Summary of the Number of States, Counties, Payams and Bomas in the Republic of South Sudan

Serial No.	Name of the State	Number of Counties	Number of Payams	Number of Bomas
1	Lakes	8	51	124
2	Northern Bahr el Ghazal	5	37	107
3	Warrap	6	41	120
4	Western Bahr el Ghazal	3	18	72
5	Central Equatoria	6	41	231
6	Eastern Equatoria	8	41	211
7	Western Equatoria	10	49	199
8	Jonglei	11	56	228
9	Upper Nile	13	54	252
10	Unity	9	37	164
Total	**10**	**79**	**425**	**1,708**

Source: LOGOSEED Documents.

On 17th April 2016, the President of the Republic of South Sudan H.E. Gen. Salva Kiir Mayardit issued a Republican Order No. 13/2016 for the creation of New Counties in the Twenty Eight (28) States in the Decentralized System of Government in the Republic of South Sudan. Abyei area was treated as an Administrative Area independent from the states. The President was exercising the powers conferred upon him under section 20 (93) of the Local Government Act 2009, read together with the Council of States Resolution No. 02/2016, dated April 15th, 2016. The names of the created Counties of the 28 States are as in Appendix II. However, more Counties were later on added due to the demand of the citizens in the areas who felt that their areas or Payams should be upgraded to the level of Counties which also got approved by the President. Afterwards the President issued another decree for creation of other four states making the total of the States in the Republic of South Sudan to be 32, and Abyei Area still remained as an Administrative Area. In another development the President of the Republic of South Sudan issued a Presidential decree abolishing the 32 States and a return to the previous 10 states as well as former counties. But Abyei, Pibor and Ruweng were made to be Administrative Areas to serve the political interests of those three areas.* It is worth mentioning that the number of the counties of 28 states rose to 233 counties, whereas the number of counties of 32 states increased to 295 counties. The 32 states and their counties are in Appendix III.

5.8. Local Government Councils in South Sudan
5.8.1. Criteria for Establishment of the Councils in South Sudan

The criteria for creation and establishment of the local government councils in South Sudan are as follows:[103]

a. Size of the territory;

b. Population;

c. Economic viability;

d. Common interest of law and communities; and

e. Administrative convenience and effectiveness.

---

103   Local Government Act, 2005. P. 15.

5.8.2. Criteria for Creation of Local Government Councils as Corporate Bodies in South Sudan

5.8.2.1. Criteria for Creation of a County Council

A County Council shall be created on the following basis:[104]

a. the size of a population of 70,000-100,000;

b. economic viability of 35%-45% of total annual budget;

c. common interest of the communities (consideration of minority or majority ethnic group cases as may be decided by South Sudan Legislative Assembly);

d. administrative convenience and effectiveness (organizational ability and ease in territorial coverage and communication access);

e. Boma the basic Administrative Unit of County shall have a population of 5,000-10,000 people;

f. about 3-4 Bomas shall constitute a Payam; and

g. about 3-4 Payams shall constitute a County.

5.8.2.2. Criteria for Creation of a City Council

A City Council shall be created on the following basis:[105]

a. The size of the population of 200,000-500,000;

b. economic viability of 75%-100% of total annual budget;

c. common interest of the communities;

d. (political decision) administrative convenience and effectiveness (strategic location);

e. the Quarterly Council of the City may have 20,000-25,000 people;

f. four (4) Quarter Councils shall constitute a Block Council; and

g. about 4-5 Block Councils constitute a City Council.

---

104   Ibid. P. 93.
105   Ibid. 93.

5.8.2.3. Criteria for Creation of a Municipal Council

Criteria for creation of a Municipal Council shall be on the following basis:[106]

a. Size of population of 100,000–300,000 people;

b. economic viability of 63%–75% of total annual budget;

c. common interest of the communities (based on growth potential);

d. administrative convenience and effectiveness (capacity of a growing Block Councils to assume the status of separate Municipal Councils);

e. the Quarter Council of a Municipality may have a population of 20,000–25,000 people;

f. four (4) Quarter Councils shall constitute a Block Council; and

g. about 4–5 Block Councils shall constitute a Municipality.

5.8.2.4. Criteria for Creation of a Town Council

Criteria for creation of a Town Council shall be on the following basis:[107]

a. the size of population of 50,000–100,000;

b. economic viability of 55%–65% of total annual budget;

c. common interest of communities based on growth potential;

d. and the administrative convenience and effectiveness (capacity of a growing rural centre to successfully manage the local council as an authority with potential to assume the status of a Town Council).

---

106   Ibid. P. 93-94.
107   Ibid. P.94.

5.8.3. Organs of the Councils in South Sudan

The organs of the local government councils are as the following:[108]

a. The Legislative Council;

b. The Executive Council; and

c. The Customary Law Council.

These local government councils exercise legislative, executive and customary judicial authority on matters and functional areas specified by law.

5.8.4. Responsibilities of the Councils in South Sudan

The responsibilities of the local government councils are as the following (LGA, 2009):

a. Regulation and maintenance of law and public order;

b. Regulation, provision and maintenance of services to the people;

c. Land administration and environmental management; and

d. Encouragement and promotion of local development and provision of access and opportunities for the people to engage in the development of their communities; and protection of the rights of the people and their interests.

5.8.5. Functions of the Executive Council of South Sudan

The Executive Council according to Article 47 (1) of the Local Government Act, 2009, is invested with the following functions:

a. Undertake the general planning and administration of the Local Government Council;

b. Provide services to the people;

c. Approve administrative policies proposed by the Legislative Council;

---

108   "What is Good Governance". UNESCAP, 2009. Accessed April 6, 2021.

d. Implement policies and by-laws passed by the Legislative Council;

e. Prepare annual budget and reports to the Legislative Council on the progress of the executive work;

f. Report to the legislative Council upon its request;

g. Initiate Acts for submission to the Legislative Council;

h. Exercise powers and competencies in Schedules of the Act; and

i. Perform functions assigned to its functional departments as specified in the Schedules of the Act.

5.9. Powers and Functions of the County Commissioner in South Sudan

The Commissioner as the head of Local Government in the County is vested with the following functions as specified by Article 52 of the Local Government Act, 2009:[109]

1. Organize the executive institutions of the County to perform their functions and duties diligently and effectively;

2. Preserve the security of the County and protect its people and its territorial integrity;

3. Maintain law and order in the County;

4. Execute policies passed and By-laws enacted by the Legislative Council, resolutions and decisions of the Executive Council;

5. Preside over the meetings of the County Executive Council;

6. Initiate legislations and amendments to the Legislative Council and assents and signs them into law;

7. Summon, adjourn or prorogue the Legislative Council in consultation with the Chairperson of the Legislative Council;

8. Mobilize and organize the general public to play an effective role in service delivery and development;

---

109   Laws of Southern Sudan. Local Government Act, 2009, pp. 32-33.

9. Coordinate the activities and functions of government, non-governmental organizations, private sector and community ventures within the County, and;

10. Perform other functions and duties as may be prescribed by law, delegated by the State Authorities or the Government of South Sudan or as may be authorized by the Legislative Council.

5.10. Powers and Functions of the Mayor in South Sudan

The Mayor as the head of the City Council or Municipal Council exercises the following functions and duties:[110]

1. Organize the executive institutions of the City or Municipality to perform their functions and duties diligently and effectively;

2. Preserve the security of the City or Municipality and protect its people and its territorial integrity;

3. Maintain law and order in the City or Municipality;

4. Execute policies passed and By-laws enacted by the Legislative Council, resolutions and decisions of the Executive Council;

5. Preside over the meetings of the City or Municipal Executive Council;

6. Initiate legislations and amendments to the Legislative Council and assents and signs them into law;

7. Summon, adjourn or prorogue the Legislative Council in consultation with the Chairperson of the Legislative Council;

8. Mobilize and organize the general public to play an effective role in service delivery and development;

9. Coordinate the activities and functions of government, non-governmental organizations, private sector and community ventures within the City or Municipal, and;

10. Perform other functions and duties as may be prescribed by law,

---

110   Ibid. pp. 35-36.

delegated by the State Authorities or the Government of South Sudan or as may be authorized by the Legislative Council.

5.11. Role of County Governments in South Sudan

The Government of the Republic of South Sudan (GRSS) is committed to improving service delivery to the population as one of the key priorities elaborated in the South Sudan Development Plan (SSDP). Counties have a key responsibility to deliver services to the population in their areas of jurisdiction. In order to effectively achieve their mandate, they must plan and budget for the execution of these services.[111]

Guidelines for the plans and preparation of the budget were prepared by the Ministry of Finance and Economic Planning and the Local Government Board to support counties in the preparation of their budgets for fiscal year (FY) 2013/14.[112]

As pertaining to the role of counties, county governments are responsible for local service delivery activities in their areas, which they must implement through their various departments of Health, Education and Water and under the overall leadership of the County Executive Director and the County Commissioner. The Counties are responsible for ensuring the functionality of various service deliveries in those and other sectors. In recognition of the key role the Counties play in service delivery, the Local Government Act 2009 Section 47.1 (e) requires County Executive Councils to prepare Annual Budgets to provide resources for those functions in Section 70 (2) of the same Act, and assigns responsibility of preparing LG annual budget to the Planning Unit. Section 83 (4) of the LG Act stipulates that "the proposed council budget shall be approved by a simple majority of the members of the

111   LOGOSEED Documents. P. 2.
112   Ibid. P. 2.

Legislative Council. On this basis LGs have a key obligation to prepare budgets"[113] for their operations every year.

A County Budget is a translation of the County's policy priorities into monetary terms. It is an annual plan of how County income and all monies received from other sources will be spent in accordance with its goals and priorities. As such it is a County's central policy instrument for setting priorities and allocating resources received, and in what it plans to achieve with them. It is through the budget process that Counties must prioritize activities they can do, and those they cannot afford.[114]

5.12. Grant Transfers to the Counties in South Sudan

The Republic of South Sudan (RSS), spearheaded by the Ministry of Finance and Economic Planning, had developed a financing framework for local services support that introduces transfers to Counties that is expected to complement the revenue that they raise.

On this basis, Counties receive three types of transfers from the State and national governments, namely:[115]

1. **County Block Grant**: the purpose of this grant is to fund core County administrative functions performed by the County Administration Department. It can also be allocated to reflect County priorities.

2. **Conditional Transfers**: The conditional transfers include the following:

    a. Sectoral salaries for education, health and water and sanitation sectors' staff.

    b. Sectoral operating for day-to-day running costs of these

---

113   Ibid. P. 2.
114   Ibid. P. 2.
115   Ibid. Pp. 3-4.

sectoral departments-budgeted by the relevant County Department in line with the guidance given by the national sector agencies in the States and County Planning, Budgeting and Reporting Guidelines.

c. Sectoral service delivery unit grants: a new capitation grant introduced for schools. States and Counties should both budget for this as a service delivery grant, and will be responsible for monitoring schools' use of the funds.

3. **Development Grants**: This includes the reformed County Development Grant (CDG) and the new Payam Development Grant (PDG) for some counties. Both CDG and PDG are discretionary development grants to fund county and Payam priorities.

5.13. County Transfers Monitoring Committees in South Sudan

All States are required to set up County Transfers Monitoring Committees (CTMCs) chaired by either the State Ministries of Finance or the State Ministries of local Government, with membership drawn from all the State Ministries that budget transfers to Counties for local service delivery as well as the State Ministry of Labour and Public Service and the Secretariat General of the States. The function of CTMCs is oversight and review of County budgets and quarterly budget performance reports. Counties are required to note that: Once the draft County budget has been prepared, it should immediately be submitted to the CTMC, pending approval by the Legislative Council. Once approved by the County Legislative Council, it again has to be submitted to the CTMC at the State for information and use as a basis for reviewing the budget performance reports. The CTMC is not supposed to change the approved county budget.[116]

---

116   Ibid. Pp. 4.

CHAPTER SIX

THE CIVIL SERVICE OF THE LOCAL GOVERNMENT COUNCIL IN SOUTH SUDAN

6.1. Composition of the Civil Service of the Local Government Council in South Sudan

The civil service of the local government councils in South Sudan comprises of the Chief Administrator of the Council; the County Executive Director; the Chief Executive Officer; the Town Clerk; Seconded Staff of the Council; and Local Staff of the Council. Each of them has functions to perform.

6.2. Chief Administrators of the Local Government Councils in South Sudan

Each Local Government Council in South Sudan is headed by an administrator from the general list of the Local Government Administrative Officers of the State and who is the head of civil service of the council. The titles of the chief administrators of the local government councils vary according to the type and status of the council and is as indicated in table 6.1 below.

Table 6.1 shows various types of the Heads and categories of Local Government Councils according to their respective status and viability in South Sudan:

	Title of the Head of the Civil Service	Type of the Council	Category of the Council
1	Chief Executive Director	City Council	A
	Chief Executive Officer	Municipal Council	A
2	Town Clerk	Town Council	B
3	Executive Director	County Council (1)	C
4	Executive Director	County Council (2)	D
5	Local Government Administrative Officer	Industrial Councils	E
6	Local Government Administrative Officer	Rural/Payam Council★	NA

Source: Local Government Act, 2009. P. 12-13.
★It is one of the levels of the Local Government Tiers but not included in the categories by the LGA 2009.

It is worth mentioning that all the Chief Administrators are equal in terms of positions as well as the Town Clerk and the Deputy Executive Director are equal in grade but are subordinates to the County Executive Director.

6.3. Powers, Functions and Duties of Chief Administrators

6.3.1. Powers and Functions of the County Executive Director

The County Executive Director is the chief administrator of the County Council appointed from the general list of Local Government Administrative Officers of the State and exercises the following powers, functions and duties (LGA, 2009):

a. Be the deputy of the County Commissioner;

b. Be the head of the civil service of the County;

c. Be the chief financial officer of the County;

d. Represent the County Commissioner in the County Council;

e. Advise the County Commissioner on all technical matters of the Council administration;

f. Oversee the public order function of the County Council;

g. Implement policy decisions and programmes of the County Council;

h. Supervise the administration and management of the County Council finances, personnel, stores, workshops, public utilities, and recreational centres, procurement and the maintenance of moveable public assets;

i. Ensure implementation and execution of the resolutions of the County Council on all matters;

j. Monitor and evaluate the programmes and activities of the County Council;

k. Supervise and coordinate the technical functions of the Council departments;

l. Conduct performance appraisal of the seconded staff and report on their work to the County Commissioner and the State Ministries concerned;

m. Develop capacity development programmes and make

recommendations for the support and technical staff and administrative officers, to the State Ministries concerned;

n. Ensure safe custody of all County Council records and funds;

o. Mobilize and organize the general public to play an effective role in service delivery and development;

p. Coordinate government, non-governmental, private and community activities and functions in the County Council; and

q. Perform functions and duties as may be prescribed by any applicable law and/or delegated by the County Commissioner.

6.3.2. The Chief Executive Officer

The Chief Executive Officer is the chief administrator of the Municipal or City Council appointed from the general list of Local Government Administrative Officers of the State and exercises the following powers, functions and duties (LGA, 2009):

a. Be the deputy of the Mayor;

b. Be the head of the civil service of the City or Municipal Council;

c. Be the chief financial officer of the City or Municipal Council;

d. Represent the Mayor in the City or Municipal Council;

e. Advise the Mayor on all technical matters of the City or Municipal Council administration;

f. Oversee the public order function of the City or Municipal Council;

g. Implement policy decisions and programmes of the City or Municipal Council;

h. Supervise the administration and management of the City or Municipal Council finances, personnel, stores, workshops, public utilities, and recreational centres, procurement and the maintenance of moveable public assets;

i.   Ensure implementation and execution of the resolutions of the City or Municipal Council on all matters;

j.   Monitor and evaluate the programmes and activities of the City or Municipal Council;

k.   Supervise and coordinate the technical functions of the City or Municipal departments;

l.   Conduct performance appraisal of the seconded staff and report on their work to the Mayor and the State Ministries concerned;

m.   Develop capacity development programmes and make recommendations for the support and technical staff and administrative officers, to the State Ministries concerned;

n.   Ensure safe custody of all City or Municipal Council records and funds;

o.   Mobilize and organize the general public to play an effective role in service delivery and development;

p.   Coordinate government, non-governmental, private and community activities and functions in the City or Municipal Council; and

q.   Perform other functions and duties as may be prescribed by any other applicable law and/or delegated by the Mayor.

6.3.3. The Town Clerk

The Town Clerk is the Chief Administrator of the Town Council appointed from the general list of Administrative Officers of the State and exercises the following powers, functions and duties (LGA, 2009):

a.   Chairperson of the Town Security Committee;

b.   Head of the Town Executive Council;

c.   Chief financial officer of the Town Council;

d.   Represent the County Commissioner in the Town Council;

e. Advise the County Commissioner on all technical matters of the Town Council administration;

f. Oversee the public order functions of the Town Council;

g. Implement policy decisions and programmes of the Town Council;

h. Supervise the administration and management of the Town Council finances, personnel, stores, workshops, public utilities, and recreational centres, procurement and the maintenance of moveable and immoveable public assets;

i. Implementation and/or execution of the resolutions of the Town Council on all matters;

j. Monitor and evaluate the programmes and activities of the Town Council;

k. Supervise and coordinate the technical functions of the Town Council departments;

l. Conduct performance appraisal of the seconded staff and report on their work to the County Commissioner and the State Ministries concerned;

m. Develop capacity development programmes and make recommendations for the support and technical staff and administrative officers, to the State Ministries concerned;

n. Ensure safe custody of all Town Council records and funds;

o. Mobilize and organize the general public to play an effective role in service delivery and development;

p. Coordinate government, non-governmental, private and community activities, functions and duties in the Town Council; and

q. Perform other functions and duties as may be prescribed by any other applicable law and/or delegated by the County Commissioner.

CHAPTER SEVEN

LOCAL GOVERNMENT PLANNING AND FINANCE IN SOUTH SUDAN

7.1. Introduction

Within the Principal of Integrated Participatory Planning, each local council should have a planning unit which is responsible for making Council plans. The preparation of the Council plans has to be based on an integrated participatory approach which has to encompass the departmental plans of all the units of the Council. The Council plans have to be made up of annual, medium and long term plans. The planning unit is charged with the preparation of all service delivery and the socio-economic development plans of the Council. Within its mandate, the planning unit makes plans for provision of basic or primary services in conformity with the State and Government of South Sudan sectoral plans and policies.

7.2. Functions and Duties of the Planning Unit

The functions and duties of the Local Government Council Planning Unit are as the following:[117]

1. Identify, analyze and prioritize the needs of the Council.
2. Prepare the Council Plan and Budget for approval by the Legislative Council.
3. Monitor and supervise the implementation of the Council Plan and Budget.
4. Coordinate and monitor the activities of all development partners in the implementation of the Councils projects.
5. Perform any other functions and duties as may be assigned to it.

7.3. Sources of Local Government Council Finance

The Local Government Council gets its funds from a combination of government grants, locally generated revenues, community contributions, grants and donations from organizations and individuals and loans in accordance with its credit worthiness or any other sources authorized by law. The funds raised by the Council from its sources are to meet its expenditures.

7.3.1. Council Local Sources of Revenue

The Local Government Councils generate revenue from the following sources:[118]

a) Taxes

i. Council property tax;

ii. Social service tax;

iii. Council land tax;

iv. Animal tax;

v. Gibana tax;

---

117   Local Government Act, 2009. P. 48.
118   Ibid. Pp. 48-51.

vi. Council sales tax;

vii. Capital gains tax;

viii.Produce tax (ushur); and

ix. Any other taxes as may be authorized by law, rules and regulations.

b) Local Rates

i.   User service charges;

ii.   License fee;

iii. Administrative fines;

iv.   Royalties;

v.   Permits;

vi.   Customary court fees and fines;

vii. Contract fees;

viii.Auction fees; and

ix.   Any other fees and charges as may be authorized by any other law, rules and regulations.

c) Local earnings from the council investments and projects.

7.3.2. Community Contributions

Each Council may mobilize resources from the community in the following forms:

a.   Labour contribution;

b.   Monetary contribution; and contribution in kind.

7.3.3. Grant-in-Aid

The Local Government Council can mobilize funds to meet its expenditure through accessing grants from governments, donors and donor agencies.

7.3.3.1. Government Grants

The Council can receive grant-in-aid from the Government of South Sudan and the State in form of the following:

a. Conditional grants;
b. Block grants;
c. Equalization grants; and
d. State support grants.

7.3.3.2. Donor Grants

Donor grants to the Council are as follows:

a. Direct financial assistance to the Local Government Council concerned;
b. Indirect financial assistance to Local Government Council concerned, channeled through donor agencies, international and national non-governmental and community based organization operating in the particular Local Government Council area; and
c. Technical assistance to the local Government Councils.

7.3.3.3. Loans

a. The Local Government Councils as corporate bodies, based on their credit worthiness, have the right to borrow; and
b. Each Council can encourage and promote the establishment of micro-finance institutions from which it can access credit facilities for its projects.

7.3.4. Local Government Development Fund

Local Government Councils are authorized to establish Local Government Development Fund which is a 'basket fund'[119] for all

---

119   Ibid. Pp. 51-52.

donations and contributions to the Local Government Councils to meet the recovery and development expenditures of the Councils. The main sources of the Local Government Development Fund are as the following:

a. Transfers from the Government of South Sudan for recovery and community development projects at the local government level;

b. Special funds allocated by the government of South Sudan and the State Governments as supplementary funds to offset Local Government Council development budget deficits;

c. National donations and contributions earmarked to fund specified socio-economic and cultural projects at the Local Government level; and

d. International donations and contributions earmarked to support Local Government recovery and development programmes.

CHAPTER EIGHT

THE TRADITIONAL AUTHORITIES OF SOUTH SUDAN

8.1. Introduction

The Traditional Authorities of South Sudan are "institutions of traditional system of governance at the State and Local government levels"[120] which are semi-autonomous authorities; administer customary law and justice; and exercise deconcentrated powers in the performance of executive functions at the local government levels within their respective jurisdictions.

In exercise of the delegated and/or deconcentrated powers, the Traditional Authorities observe, respect and adhere to the Act of Rights enshrined in the National South Sudan and State Constitutions.

---

120   Ibid. P. 75.

8.2. Types of Traditional Authority in South Sudan

In the Republic of South Sudan "there are two types of Traditional Authority"[121]: the Kingdoms and the Chiefdoms.

1. **Kingdoms:** They are centralized monarchical systems of rule whose institutions perform local government functions while maintaining their status as the institutions of the kingdoms in the given states in South Sudan. Kingdoms are in some specific areas of one or more counties. Kingdoms are divided into chieftainships; sub-chieftainships; and headman ships and are recognized as self existing traditional systems.

2. **Chiefdoms:** They are decentralized system of rule which perform traditional and local government functions covering territorial area of counties where the traditional authorities are organized on the basis of lineages and clans which are divided into sub-chieftainships and headman ships. They are traditional community authority through which people rule themselves. Chiefdoms are established in accordance with the provisions of the Local Government Act and regulations. They are autonomous within the County or Town Council and they organize their traditional institutions of governance and choose their leaders to administer themselves. The territories and boundaries of Chiefdoms are determined and demarcated by local legislation and regulations. The seat of each Chiefdom is in the administrative headquarters of the local government unit concerned.

8.3. Decentralization of Chiefdoms in South Sudan

Chiefdoms are decentralized into Paramount Chieftainship, Head Chieftainship and Executive Chieftainship.

---

121   Ibid. Pp. 75-76.

The Paramount Chieftainship is comprised of Paramount Chief as the head and all the Head Chiefs of the Chieftainships who administer their area and run traditional judicial courts.

Head Chieftainships is comprised of Head Chief of the Chieftainship and the Executive Chiefs of the Chieftainship.

Executive Chieftainships comprise of the Executive Chief as the head and Sub-Chiefs. Where there are two or more Chieftainships in a Boma, the most senior chief becomes the head of the Chieftainship.

The powers, functions and duties of the Paramount, Head and Executive Chieftainships are determined by local legislation and regulations.

8.4. Criteria for the Establishment of Chieftainships
8.4.1. Executive Chieftainship
The criteria for the establishment of Executive Chieftainship are as follows:[122]

a. A Headmanship with a population of two hundred and fifty to three hundred people.

b. A Sub-Chieftaincy consisting of five to six Headmanships with a population of one thousand two hundred and fifty to one thousand five hundred people.

c. An Executive Chieftainship consisting of five to six Sub-Chieftainships with a population of six thousand two hundred and fifty to nine thousand people.

d. A Head Chieftainship consisting of five to six Executive Chieftainships; and

e. A Paramount Chieftainship consisting of five to six Head Chieftainships.

---

122   Ibid. P. 77.

8.4.2. Election of the Chiefs

Criteria for the election of Chiefs are as the following:[123]

a. Chiefs are elected according to conventional electoral system or selected according to traditional practices.

b. The Paramount Chief is elected by all the Chiefs including the Head Chiefs and Executive Chiefs in the County.

c. The Head Chief is elected by the Executive Chiefs and Sub-Chiefs in his or her jurisdiction.

d. The Executive Chief is elected by the Sub-Chiefs and all the people, including women who are eligible to vote in his her jurisdiction.

e. All the selected Chiefs who Chieftainships constitutes the institutions of governance of Kingdoms assume offices according to their customs and practices which are inconformity with the provisions of the Act and any other applicable law.

8.5. Council of Traditional Authority Leaders

The Constitution of South Sudan Article 175 (2) provides for the establishment of Council of Traditional Authority Leaders and State Council of Traditional Authority Leaders at the national and the State levels respectively.

The composition, functions and duties of the State Council of Traditional Leaders are determined by the relevant State legislation.

The Council of Traditional Authority Leaders, as a source of legislation, is the custodian of the customs and traditions of the people of South Sudan.

The council of Traditional Authority Leaders at the national level is composed of forty five members as follows:[124]

a. Four members are elected representatives from each State

---

123   Ibid. P. 78.
124   Ibid. P. 79.

Council of Traditional Authority Leaders and at least one should be a woman; and

b. Five members are appointed by the President after consultation with the relevant authorities.

8.6. Functions and Duties of the South Sudan Council of Traditional Authority Leaders

8.6.1. Functions of the South Sudan Council of Traditional Authority Leaders

The functions of the South Sudan Council of Traditional Leaders are as follows:[125]

a. Provide a forum for dialogue with all levels of government on matters of customs and traditions of the people of South Sudan;

b. Intervene to resolve inter-tribal disputes by applying customary and traditional conflict resolution mechanisms;

c. Foster peace building on resolution of conflicts through mediation and other conciliatory mechanisms;

d. Advise all levels of Government on matters of traditions and customs of the people of South Sudan; and

e. Perform other functions and duties as provided by the Act and any other applicable law or regulations.

8.6.2. The Duties of the South Sudan Council of Traditional Authority Leaders

They duties of the South Sudan Council of Traditional Leaders are as the following:[126]

a. Organize regular sessions of dialogue with stakeholders on customs and traditions;

b. Initiate, establish and disseminate processes and traditional

---

125   Ibid. Pp. 80-81.
126   Ibid. Pp. 8o-81.

conflict resolution mechanisms for interventions in the settlement of inter-tribal disputes; and

c. Establish, promote and maintain linkages and peaceful co-existence with all traditional leaders and nationalities across South Sudan.

8.6.3. Recommendations for Support of Traditional Authorities

The following are recommendations for the support of the traditional authorities:

a. Traditional authorities should be supported through on-going capacity building and adequate dissemination of the new laws. Both traditional authorities and local government officials should be helped to develop a clearer understanding of the links between county, state and central levels of government in order to be able to operate optimally within these new state structures.

b. The government should be supportive to work with traditional authorities.

c. Gender mainstreaming and gender equality are new themes in South Sudanese governance policy, on-going consistent support is needed for them to become strongly rooted in South Sudanese society. Donors should provide guidance and resources in this regard.

d. Efforts and Projects in support of decentralized democratic governance should be properly documented and stored, and lessons learned database created on forms of local governance and possible ways to integrate traditional authorities and cultural values into states structures. This would be useful for future South Sudan reference, as well as to inform other states facing such challenges and dissemination lessons.

CHAPTER NINE

THE LOCAL GOVERNMENT BOARD

9.1. Introduction

The Local Government Board (LGB) is established in accordance with the provisions of Article 173 (3) of the Constitution of South Sudan, 2011. At the initial stage of the establishment of LGB, particularly at the interim period from 2005 to 2011 before the independence of South Sudan, LGB was from time to time assigned mandatory executive functions and powers for the discharge of the local government affairs.

9.2. Mandatory Executive Functions and Powers of Local Government Board

The mandatory executive functions of the LGB are as the following:

a. To review and formulate local government policies and legal frameworks; and

b. To recommend and coordinate the establishment of minimum standards and uniform norms for service delivery in accordance with respective relative provisions of Schedules of the Constitution.

9.3. Functions and Duties of the Local Government Board

In addition to the mandatory executive functions above, LGB has also the following functions and duties:[127]

a. Make recommendations for organization and establishment of Local Government Council;

b. Recommend to the President the formation of a High Technical Committee for the creation and establishment of Local Government Councils in the ten states of South Sudan in accordance with criteria set forth in Article 173 (4) of the Constitution of South Sudan, 2011;

c. Prepare Warrants of Establishment showing the status, administrative jurisdiction and the boundary of each Local Government Council for signature by the President;

d. Review and recommend on the performance and administration of local government affairs of each Local Government Council in consultation with State Governments and report its findings to the State Governors and the President for consideration; and

e. Research and recommend the development of relevant concepts, principles and workable policy framework of local government.

9.4. Functions and Duties of Local Government Board by the Directives of the President

The LGB upon the directives of the President prepare administrative circulars to regulate the status, conditions and quality of services being delivered to the people as follows:

---

127   Ibid. Pp. 82-84.

a. Determine the appropriate transitional arrangements and mechanisms for the smooth transformation of the existing Local Government Councils from their current rudimentary stages to integrated modern local authorities;

b. Promote the adoption of relevant models for local government planning resource mobilization and management, service delivery and local development programmes;

c. Set national standards for recruitment, training management and performance appraisal of the Local Government staff;

d. Review local government financial resources and recommend relevant models for grants allocation and disbursement; and

e. Recommend the adoption of common norms and values to orient local government administration to be more responsive to the people in service delivery.

9.5. Areas of Assistance by the Local Government Board

The LGB assists in the coordination of the local government affairs in the following ways:

a. The establishment of good inter-governmental linkages to harmonize the working relationships between the People's Local Government Councils and government institutions at the State and Government of South Sudan levels; and

b. The development of model local government programmes for service delivery at the local levels which may be adopted for implementation by the State Ministries of Local Government and the Local Government Councils.

9.6. Local Government Board Achievements

The Local Government Board, as per mandate bestowed by the Constitution and elaborated by the Local Government Act 2009, is responsible for reviewing and formulating local government policies and legal frameworks, regulating systems and mechanisms for improving service delivery to the people and coordinating local government affairs in support of State ministries of Local Government and local Government councils.

LGB was established in 2006. The LGB originates from the experience of the SPLM Secretariat of Local Government before the Comprehensive Peace Agreement (CPA) of 2005. In response to a prospect of peace and with support from international partners, a focal point team was formed by the SPLM Secretariat of Local Government of New Sudan and deliberated on a Local Government Framework, taking account of local administration and governance experience in Southern Sudan in the 1950s and 1970s to early 1980s. The Local Government Framework was finalized in 2005, following the signing of the CPA, and provided a base document for the drafting of a Local Government Bill. The Local Government Act, was enacted in April 2009, one of the first legislations adopted by the Government of Southern Sudan (GoSS) in the wake of CPA. Among the achievements of the LGB are the following:[128]

a. In 2007-2008, the LGB conducted screening examinations and identified 1,583 Local Government Administrative Officers (LGAOs) across Southern Sudan, who were considered to have sufficient qualifications to carry out the duties. Training these officers and supporting counties to undergo annual planning and budgeting, one of fundamental functions of a government entity, were the first tasks of the LGB.

b. With the passage of the LGB Act 2009, the LGB began focusing on the implementation of the Act. Against this background and in the line with the overall mandate of the LGB, the Directorate

---

128   Local Government Board Report, January 2015. Pp-1-5.

of Planning and Programme has been responsible for improving professional knowledge and skills of LGAOs, developing and strengthening institutions and systems of local governments and coordinating and facilitating activities with the State Ministry of Local Governments and partner organizations.

c.   Training of LGAOs: Five three-weeks training sessions were organized in 2008-2009 with the support from UNDP. A total of 274 LGAOs were selected and trained in these sessions on a range of topics including the Local Government Act 2009, basics of local government administration, participatory planning and budgeting, basics of financial management, facilitation skills and gender equity. The trainings were conducted as Training of Trainers (ToTs) with the aim of deploying three LGAOs in each county and SMoLG headquarters, who were then expected to train other LGAOs and staff, while undertaking core responsibilities of the counties. 79 of these trained LGAOs were selected in late 2011 for another three week training focusing on public financial management, with support from UNDP and CBTF.

.   In light of the experience gained from the initial trainings, the LGB conducted training needs assessment and developed a long-term training plan in 2009, consisting of three categories of courses: orientation, induction and specialized training. Training materials were developed for orientation and induction with the technical assistance of German Development Cooperation (GIZ). Orientation and induction courses were then conducted in 2010-2012 with assistance of GIZ, USAID and CBTF.

d.   County Participatory Planning and Budgeting: Through the LGAOs who had received foundation trainings in 2008-2009, the LGB began guiding the counties to prepare a strategic plan and annual plan and budget in 2008. Several draft planning and budgeting guidelines that had been used and piloted during the initial period were rationalized into "Participatory Planning and Budgeting Guide for Local Governments in South Sudan," which was formerly adopted by the LGB in January 2011. Classroom sessions and hands-on guidance for the 79 counties were carried out in 2010-2012 with the assistance of UNDP and USAID. However, the technical assistance efforts were suspended in 2012, affected by the austerity measures introduced in early 2012 and donors' withdrawal of support to local governments. Since mid-2013, there has been renewed attention to county development planning and annual budgeting, owing to Local Governance and Service Delivery Project (LOGOSEED) financed by the World Bank and some bilateral donors. In parallel, the Local Service Support (LSS) was initiated, led by the Ministry of Finance and Economic Planning (MoFEP) with the active participation of the LGB and four other ministries (Health, General Education, Water and Irrigation and Public Service and HRD). The LSS has been instrumental in mobilizing attention and resources for systematic guiding counties on planning and budgeting as well as budget execution.

e. Commissioners' Forums: The concept of Commissioners' Forum in the ten states was derived from the experience of the Governors' Forum that had started in 2006 and became an annual event. In 2010, the LGB, with support from UNDP and UNMISS, coordinated with the ten state governments to organize a Commissioners' Forum in each state. They were the first organized state-level platforms for exchanging experiences and discussing policy directions with respect to local governance and administration. The ten Commissioners' Forums generated lively discussions and a great deal of enthusiasm for improving policy, institutional and operating environment for the counties. The second round of the Commissioners' forums was held in 2012 with the assistance from UNDP and technical logistical support from USAID and UNMISS. The LGB, the state governments and counties intend to institutionalize the Commissioners' Forums as an annual event preceding the Governors' Forum, but lack of systematic funding and logistical support has been a major constraint.

f. Induction Guide for Local Government Councillors: The 79 counties across South Sudan recognized by the national government are based on counties that had been established under the system of local government introduced by the Civil Authority of the New Sudan (CANS) of the SPLA/M in the mid-1990s. Two key issues remain pending in respect of the formal establishment of Local Government Councils as stipulated in the Local Government Act 2009. First, the process for warrants of establishment to be issued by the President based on technical consideration is yet to start. Second, elections of Local Government Councillors have not taken place. As a temporary arrangement, the state governments have established Local Government Councils with members appointed by the Governor in most of the counties. In many cases, the appointments are based on selection from communities, which serves meeting a minimum requirement for democratic representation at the local level. "The Councilors' Induction Guide" was prepared in 2011 with UNDP's technical assistance. The guide was designed to serve two purposes:

i. To guide LGAOs and partner organizations for conducting and induction workshop for Councillors; and

ii. For the Councillors to use it as an orientation and reference material. Funding and technical support are required for systematic implementation of this guide; needless to say, the Councillors gaining good understanding on their roles and responsibilities are an indispensable component of local governance.

g. Local Government Public Financial Management Manual and Human Resources Management Manual: A Local Government Public Financial Management (PFM) Manual was prepared in 2012 and finalized in 2013 by the joint efforts of the Ministry of Finance and Economic Planning (MoFEP) and LGB with support from CBTF. Throughout 2013 state and county officials/staff responsible for PFM were trained based on the Manual by the Government Accountancy Training Centre (GATC) with CBTF funding. The LGB also closely coordinated with the Ministry of Public Service and Human Resource Development (MoPS&HRD) in developing a standard organizational structure and HR policy for local governments. These efforts provided building blocks of the Local Service Support (LSS), the umbrella initiative led by the MoFEP mentioned above.

h. Coordination with Partners: Most of the above mentioned activities were supported by partners coordinated by the LGB. The coordination mechanism was originally introduced in 2011 and has been recently revised under LSS, with the support of LOGOSEED, and the World Bank-funded project.

i. Local Service Support (LSS) and Local Governance and Service Delivery Project (LOGOSEED): The Local Service Support (LSS) continued in FY 2014/15 on the basis of the Joint Plan of Action (JPA) endorsed by the Undersecretaries of Economic

Planning, LGB, Health, General Education, Water and Irrigation and Public Service & HRD in July 2013. Priority action areas for FY 2014/15 were discussed and endorsed by the LSS Task Force in June 2014 are as follows:

i. To ensure a coherent set of policies and institutions for decentralized service delivery.

ii. To ensure adequate sector management of local service delivery.

iii. To ensure adequate and equitably distributed staffing at LG and facility level.

iv. To ensure adequate, timely and equitably distributed funding for LGs and facilities.

v. To hold local government to fiduciary standards.

vi. To ensure transparency and accountability for service delivery.

. Five Technical Working Groups (TWGs) have been established to guide and coordinate activities in these areas. They are: LG PFM & HR, LG TWG, Primary Education TWG, Health TWG, and Rural Water & Sanitation TWG. The LGB is responsible for the LG TWG and is also represented in the other TWGs to provide inputs from practical experiences in local governments and to ensure coordination with LG TWG.

. Local Governance and Service Delivery Project (LOGOSEED) implemented jointly with the MoFEP and LGB was started in 2013 and continued until FY 2016/17. LOGOSEED is aligned with the LSS and its Project Management Committee (PMC), a technical-level body of the government, functions as another, sixth TWG of the LSS. The project has four components:

.

i. Block Grant for Payam Development (PDG);

ii. Community Engagement;

iii. Institutional Strengthening of Counties; and

iv. Project Management.

. In FY 2014/15 the project was active in 3 counties each in Lakes and Western Equatoria and 2 counties each in Warrap and Eastern Equatoria. 2 counties each in Upper Nile and Jonglei that received support in 2013 were expected to rejoin the project once the security is restored in the states. Government delegations to these two states were planned for February 2015 to conduct assessment. The project was expected to reach all ten states by FY 2016/17.

j. Training of Local Government Administrative Officers (LGAOs): At the moment, LOGOSEED was the only project that provided systematic capacity development support at state and county levels. Their focuses were PFM (that includes planning/budgeting, procurement, contract management, financial management and reporting), engineering (that includes designing facilities, preparing bills of quantities and bidding documents and supervision of construction works) and environmental and social safeguards. 10 counties (in Lakes, Western Equatoria, Warrap and Eastern Equatoria) received the intensive technical assistance of LOGOSEED.

. Another project, technical assistance for local government PFM and payroll systems, started with support from the European Union (EU) in mid-2014. This TA (referred to as EU TAPP) trained state and county officials/staff across South Sudan on the implementation of the LG PFM Manual and counties' own payroll systems (i.e. detached from the state management systems). The EU TAPP was for 18 months, or until early 2016.

While LOGOSEED was gradually to cover more states and counties, the total number of counties supported was not to be more than 55 counties in FY 2016/17 as per the plan. This means that the comprehensive support for looking after all counties similar to the one offered by EU TAPP was to be necessary after early 2016. As county transfers of the national government not only for operations and salaries but also for development through County Development Grant (CDG) was to continue, such support was crucial for ensuring proper transfer for the Government of the Republic of South Sudan (GRSS) grants to the counties and responsible uses of the grants by the counties.

. At the same time, training on dimensions other than PFM was to be re-initiated, capitalizing on the orientation and induction courses conducted in 2010-2012. Knowledge on public policy and strategic planning as well as practical skills on county administration, office management, human resource management, internal and external communications and facilitating community/citizen initiatives required another focus and coordinated approach. Organizing training with specialized institutions abroad and scholarship programmes was required for some of these subjects.

k. Training of Local Government Councillors: The Induction Guide for Councillors prepared in 2011 was yet to be implemented systematically. With the completion of the LG PFM Manual in 2013 and as the counties were guided not only on budgeting but also on execution, Councillors were oriented on key PFM concepts and principles as well as other dimensions of council responsibilities so that they are enabled to provide meaningful and effective oversight of county's executive tasks.

l. Institutionalizing Commissioners' Forums: The Commissioners'

Forums were organized in the ten states twice so far, in 2010 and 2012, as mentioned above. Ideally the Forums should have been held every year, preceding the annual Governors' Forum. This was to ensure that issues and ideas at county level were fed into the national-level forum of the state leaders, contributing to the deepening of democratic and decentralized governance that was much needed in South Sudan. The predictability of annual state-level events for county leaders and officials was also to help in instilling discipline and integrity in day-to-day management of county affairs. Support from partners was required for institutionalizing the Commissioners' Forums till the time the state governments themselves were able to finance and organize the events.

m. Operational Support: Many counties across the country, not to mention those that were affected during the crisis that erupted in December 2013, were faced with operational constraints in terms of power supply, sufficient office space, and office equipment including computers, printers and photocopiers, supplies, computers skills, staff accommodation among others. In the past UNDP and USAID provided support in this area to some extent. LOGOSEED has provided "tool kits" of equipment including solar panels and motorcycles to participating counties. Also, access to rural counties and Payam remained an enormous challenge particularly during the rainy season. These rudimentary but important issues needed to be addressed by the national government with support from partners so that adequate resources have to be allocated for addressing operational capacity bottlenecks.

CHAPTER TEN

LOCAL GOVERNMENT PROJECTS SUPPORTED BY PARTNERS

10.1. Introduction

There were a number of projects for service delivery implemented by the donors and partners in some of the counties in South Sudan with the oversight of the Local Government Board. Among them, one of these projects was the Local Governance and Service Delivery Project (LOGOSEED). The other projects were the ones implemented by German Development Cooperation (GIZ), Skills for South Sudan, UNDP and others. Their details are as hereunder.

10.2. Skills for Southern Sudan

With funding from DFID, Skills for Southern Sudan from 2002-2006 facilitated the Local Government Secretariat in training of Local Government Administrative Officers in the liberated areas of the New Sudan. Some of these Officers were trained as ToTs and others were trained in local government administration and public finance.

10.3. UNDP Assistance to Local Government Administration

While negotiations were going on between the Sudan Government and the Sudan People's Liberation Movement/Army in Naivasha-Kenya, UNDP started to support the New Sudan Local Government Secretariat from 2003 to 2006 by funding the activities of the Focal Point in 2003 which later on got transformed into Technical Team. The activities of the Team covered the drafting of the Local Government Act, Structure of the Local Government in southern Sudan, Study on existing local government structures in the New Sudan, and Study of Local Government Systems in Ethiopia and Uganda.

UNDP also had programmes to support decentralized democratic governance in South Sudan. One of them focused on the role of traditional authorities and the other was on empowering women. The study on traditional authority stressed the need to incorporate traditional authorities in local governance because of the historical legitimacy they enjoy.[129]

There were other UNDP Programmes to support decentralized democratic governance and covered:

a. Support for the Development Policies and Legislation for Responsive, Accountable and Equitable Local Government in southern Sudan which was implemented in 2005 with funding of USD200,000. The project entailed conduct of formal consultations with traditional authorities in southern Sudan to elicit their ideas on traditional structures, authorities and systems of the communities to facilitate decentralization and

---

129   Down loads_lessons_from_local_governance_programmes. P. 3.

the incorporation of these into the new local government and state structures.

b. Strategy for Mainstreaming Gender Empowerment in Local Government in southern Sudan run from 2006-2008 with USD485,000 funding. This project aimed at empowering local women to take their place in local government within the democratization of southern Sudan. It focused on the institutionalization of gender awareness, gender sensitivity and the incorporation of gender criteria within local governance structures.

c. Traditional authorities and indigenous cultural systems had provided the only constant structures of governance throughout the history of southern Sudan. 'Traditional authorities know their people, their needs and the challenges of environment. They have always provided leadership and received popular legitimacy' (Soux, 2010: 21). The Government to work with chiefs and to incorporate them in local governance and ensure effective participation of local communities. Crucially, this process of sharing governance responsibility at local level would foster the creation of a common Southern Identity to unite diverse tribes. By working with traditional authorities one maintains comfortable and legitimate structures that have the capability to rally the population towards peace and development. Education and economic development will provide modernization mechanisms in these communities (Soux, 2010: 21-22).

10.4. Recovery and Rehabilitation Programme
The mid-term and final evaluations of the Recovery and Rehabilitation Programme (RRP), implemented in five states from

2005-2010, highlighted numerous challenges in this respect. The RRP was a USD 57 million programme funded by the European Commission, administered by UNDP and implemented through NGO consortia. The RRP was explicitly designed as a transitional programme, combining quick recovery impacts within the institutional development of local government. The mid-term and final evaluation of the RRP noted that sizable outputs were achieved, particularly in service delivery infrastructure. But they found that the programme was less effective in institutional development. As a result, the service delivery outputs were not sustainable and there was insufficient capacity to maintain them after the programme ended.[130]

10.5. European Union Technical Assistance for Sub-national Capacity Building in Payroll and PFM (EU TAPP)

This was a project implemented by EU TAPP from August 2014 to the end of July 2016 by Ecorys and VNG.[131] The objectives and components of the project are as hereunder.

10.5.1. The objectives and Components of the Project

The objectives and Components of EU TAPP project were:

a. The Technical Assistance for Sub national Capacity Building in Payroll and Public Financial Management (PFM) was a three-year project funded by the European Union. The wider objective of the project was to strengthen public financial management at central, state and local level in South Sudan. The specific objective was to increase the capacity of local governments to

130   File///c:/ASUS/Down loads/Local Governance in South Sudan_ Overview_ GSDRC.html. Iffat Idris, December 2018. P. 9.
131   http://www.vng-international.nl/blog/projects/south-sudan-assis-tance-for-sub-national-capacity-building-in-payroll-and-public-financial-manage-ment-eu-tapp/. P. 9.

implement and execute existing policies and directives in the fields of payroll and PFM in all ten States of South Sudan.

b. The main components of the EU TAPP project were:

   i. Supporting local governments in meeting the requirements of the local government PFM manual;

   ii. Providing State level support for analysis of current payrolls;

   iii. Supporting county administration departments to properly manage payroll;

   iv. Supporting the establishment and operation of a County Transfer Monitoring Committee (CTMC).

10.5.2. Lessons Learned from the Project

The lessons learned from the project of EU TAPP were as hereunder:

a. The project ensured that the skills conveyed were applied in a daily context.

b. The use of a standardized capacity building approach mitigated problems regarding staff transfers. If a staff member is transferred from one county to another, the same training will have been received by that officer.

c. Payroll management system was difficult for various reasons:

   i. lack of electricity or hard wares low ICT skills of the payroll staff;

   ii. lack of knowledge about how to split the county payroll from the State payroll;

   iii. lack of clarity over the staff roles; and

   iv. lack of accurate data ready to mitigate to payroll software.

d. Complicated systems and reports do not work in a context where both equipment as well as capacity for using and interpreting the system is inadequate. However, building accountability and transparency mechanisms is essential in building a financial management system, especially in a country with high fiduciary risks such as South Sudan. In response to this, the EU–TAPP team developed a variety of simple, feedback mechanisms. These include a grant-tracking tool (GTT) which was developed and piloted in Western Equatoria State: it comprised a set of excel templates designed to capture records of grant transfers, budgets and actual receipts revealing any gaps and discrepancies.

e. There was increased understanding of PFM and their role in the process, and could improve transparency and accountability.

f. When the roll out of the payroll ICT systems turned out to be too ambitious, the team worked with local officials ensuring accurate nominal and payrolls on both State and county level, and creating reform readiness.

10.6. Oxfam Within and Without the State (WWS) Governance Programme

In 2015 Oxfam produced a brief listing lessons learned from implementation of the Within and Without the State (WWS) Governance initiative in South Sudan. This has been running since 2012 in the States of Lakes and Western Equatoria, and its focus was on strengthening the citizen-state relationship to bring about improved participation, transparency, accountability, gender equality and peace building.

The 2015 brief identified six lessons, but the one with most relevance for local governance was probably the first: work with existing state structures rather than inventing parallel systems. The Local Government Act 2009 has provisions for the establishment of County Legislative Councils: These are meant to supervise the executive council, ensure delivery of social services, approve budgets, and promote human rights and democracy. These were not functioning when WWS began. Oxfam WWS implementing partner CEPO had already begun promoting community public forums, but in the second year of WWS began lobbying for establishment of CLCs. As of July 2015 there were functioning CLCs in all eight counties of Lakes State. CEPO also delivered trainings on budget tracking to ensure CLCs could carry out their assigned role.

Similarly, to support local development, Oxfam partner SUTCO set up two Community Accountability Committees (CACs) to gather and convey the concerns of the community. Their role was also to monitor public expenditure at county and state level, and identify community needs so these could be reflected in area of development plans. While the CACs were functioning well, they had no official mandate from the state to operate and thus faced challenges from the public. LGA 2009 contains provisions for Boma/ Payam Development Committees. SUTCO therefore applied for CACs to be changed to Boma/Payam Committees as this would make them officially sanctioned and facilitate their functioning. Under WWS, specific trainings were delivered for members on budget tracking, how to liaise with Payams, how to forward cases to the Human Rights Commission or Anti Corruption Commission, and on leadership, communication and conflict resolution.

10.7. South Sudan Recovery Fund

The South Sudan Recovery Fund (SSRF) was established in 2008 to expedite delivery of recovery assistance and bridge the gap between short-term humanitarian aid and long-term development efforts. Implementation arrangements included the Government of South Sudan, UN agencies, the World Bank and donors (GoSS & UNDP, 2012: 29). While not directly focused on local governance, a 2012 assessment of SSRF identifies a number of lessons that are relevant to local governance programming:

a. A coherent theory of change is the essential programme foundation; providing strategic framework, defining the implementation modalities required and for resource allocations.

b. A theory of change is different from political imperatives confronting stake holders, and from their individual interests and incentives. It is important that these issues be separated, and addressed accordingly.

c. The State has the primary responsibility for the protection and security of its citizens. Vacuums occur when the State is not visibly present in their daily lives, its legitimacy is not recognized or respected, and where the State is unable to deliver core public goods and services.

d. Stabilization programmes are effective when implemented through State-led processes that align resource allocation, with priorities from State recovery strategies and the political consensus between national and international stake holders.

e. Bypassing Government to deliver basic services undermines the legitimacy and credibility of the State, over the medium term. Care must be taken that service delivery through non-state entities does not replace the State, and is integrated into State priorities.

10.8. Local Governance and Service Delivery Project

Local Governance and Service Delivery Project locally known as LOGOSEED, is the commonly used term for the Local Governance and Service Delivery Project. It is a project of the Government of the Republic of South Sudan (GRSS). The first project of its kind, LOGOSEED aimed to improve governance provision of services at the local level through capacity building for the planning, management and oversight of development activities in both communities and counties. The Payam Development Grant (PDG) was disbursed for this purpose so that counties and communities can practice knowledge and skills on actual development works through "learning by doing."[132]

10.8.1. Components of Local Governance and Service Delivery Project

LOGOSEED consisted of four components:[133]

1. Block grants for Payam Development used for small infrastructural projects in line with local governments and community responsibilities.

2. Community engagement through which citizens participate in selecting their priorities, planning and overseeing implementation.

3. Institutional strengthening that supports capacity building for local governments planning and budgeting, procurement, engineering, contract management, environmental and social safeguards, financial management, and monitoring and evaluation functions.

4. Management arrangements for the three components above, comprising of the Project Monitoring Unit (PMU) in support of the Ministry of Finance and Economic Planning (MoFEP) and Local Government Board (LGB) and State Coordination Offices located in the State Ministries of Local Government.

The Payam Development Grants (PDGs) are used for local

---

132   The Republic of South Sudan, Ministry of Finance and Economic Planning & Local Government Board, Local Governance and Service Delivery Project, December 2014.
133   Ibid.

public as well as economic infrastructure such as water, sanitation, storm water, health, education, markets, livestock and irrigation. The project thus addresses dire needs among communities in South Sudan. Joint County and Community Management of the grants provides opportunity for the officials to develop skills in procurement, planning, budgeting and financial management, social and safeguards management and communication. The communities learn to articulate their needs, build consensus on their priorities, monitor the projects and implement some of them.[134]

The projects are implemented through a participatory process and bottom-up approach. The process involves the communities in the selection projects as well as project sites. Boma Development Committees (BDCs) and Payam Development Committees (PDCs) take lead at this stage, acting as links between the county and the community.

The direct benefits expected from the Project include greater access to basic services, better leaning environment leading to higher school enrollment and better health. In addition it fulfills the broader objective of making the 'government felt' in the rural areas.

LOGOSEED implementation was started in four states of Lakes, Western Equatoria, Eastern Equatoria and Warrap. The Projects aimed at covering 40 counties in all the 10 states in five years. Five criteria are considered in the process of selecting counties: population, accessibility, security, similar on-going assistance and basic administrative capacity. Within the participating counties, the Payams are divided into two groups that will participate in alternating years over a two-year PDG project cycle. The counties will be audited after the PDG implementation. The audit results will determine whether or not the county can receive the next grant.[135]

---

134   Ibid.
135   Ibid.

This project was implemented from 2013/14 fiscal year to 2017/18 fiscal year. Funding for this project was from the World Bank and the Government of Denmark.

The other project is the Strengthening Local Governance and Resilience in South Sudan which was implemented by German Development Cooperation (GIZ). This project was implemented from 2007 to 2017.

10.8.2. LOGOSEED Small Infrastructure Projects

LOGOSEED has completed three years of operation as a development project. Through a small infrastructure projects, the initiative was to make the presence of the Government felt at the local level. It was also transforming the communities through extensive engagement. During the FY 2015/16, the Project became active in three new states-Western Bahr el Ghazal, Northern Bahr el Ghazal and Central Equatoria as they were known then. This was in addition to the four states in which it was already active: Lakes, Western Equatoria, Warrap and Eastern Equatoria. The number of Payam Projects (project funded by the Payam Development Grant [PDG]) implemented rose from 32 to 221 from FY 2014/15 to FY 2015/16. The projects were at an advanced stage of completion by the end of the financial year.[136]

The Project scaled up geographically, undertaking community engagement activities in 22 counties. During the engagement activities completed in August 2016, 61 Payam Development Committees (PDCs) and 333 Boma Development Committees (BDCs) were formed. The process gave the communities an opportunity to

---

136   The Republic of South Sudan. Ministry of Finance and Planning and Local Government Board. Local Governance and Service Delivery Project. July 20 to June 2016, Annual Report, Abridged Version. P. 03.

determine the Payam projects that would be implemented.[137]

Project implementation during the year was however not without challenges. These included the variance between the official exchange rate and the parallel market; the attendant inflation resulting from the repealing of exchange rate controls; funding challenges, county staff mobility after the creation of 28 states and increased number of counties, and, insecurity in some Project areas.[138] The LOGOSEED/LGDSP was a five year project being implemented by the Ministry of Finance and Planning and the Local Government Board in the Republic of South Sudan. The project was funded with a credit from the World Bank with additional funding from the Government of Denmark.

The Project aimed to support improvements in local governance and service delivery by strengthening community engagement and local government capacities in the planning, implementation and oversight of local development activities.

10.8.3. Achievements Accrued from the Components of LOGOSEED Project from Financial Year July 2015 to June 2016

The achievements accrued from the LOGOSEED Project are as follows:

a. Component 1: The Payam Development Grant (PDG):
Thirteen new counties from seven states were selected to participate in the project. These include Juba, Yei River, Magwi, Kapoeta North, Rumbek Centre, Aweil East, Aweil North, Tonj North, Nzara, Maridi, Mundri East, Wau and Jur River.[139]

Communities prioritized a total of 221 Payam projects for funding in the financial year. The priority projects largely

---

137   Ibid. p. 03.
138   Ibid. p. 03.
139   Ibid. p. 03.

consisted of boreholes, primary healthcare units and primary schools. The first tranche of the PDG funds, totaling SSP 132,710,688 (equivalent to approximately USD $3.69m) was disbursed in May 2016. Table 10.1 opposite provides the PDG allocations and while Table 10.2, provides details of the allocations and project categories. At 45%, the water sector leads in the number of projects; while education was second at 18% followed by health at 9% (health embodies sanitation which has high numbers as latrines are provided with very permanent facility constructed).[140]

---

140   Ibid. p. 03.

Table 10.1 Shows Payam Development Grant Allocation to Counties

County	Number of Payams	Payam Allocation FY: 2015/16 (in USD)	Total Allocation for Payams (in USD)	County Allocation for Operations FY 2015/16 (in USD)	Total Allocation FY 2015/16 (in USD)
Rumbek East	4	212,960	851,840	7,000	858,840
Yirol West	4	178,906	715,623	7,000	722,623
Wulu	2	140,607	281,214	7,000	288,214
Ibba	3	96,787	290,362	7,000	297,362
Mvolo	3	111,270	333,809	7,000	340,809
Gogrial West	4	422,898	1,691,592	7,000	1,698,592
Twic	3	473,672	1,421,016	7,000	1,428,016
Kapoeta East	3	397,106	1,137,319	7,000	1,144,319
Ikwoto	3	195,680	587,040	7,000	594,040
Total		2,211,886	7,309,815	63,000	7,372,815

Source: The Republic of South Sudan, Ministry of Finance and Planning and Local Government Board, Local Governance and Service Delivery Project. July 20 to June 2016, Annual Report, Abridged Version. P. 014.

Table 10.2: Payam Development Grant Project Categories

Payan Project Description	WES			LAKES		EES		WARRAP		Totals
	Ibba	Mvolo	Wulu	Rumbek East	Yirol West	Ikwoto	Kapoeta	Gogrial West	Twic	
P/S Classroom Blocks	3	5	2	1	2	4	3	13	6	39
P/S VIP Latrines	4	3	2	1	2	4	3	9	4	32
Borehole Drilling	3		4	10	21	1	19	17	24	99
Solar Panel on PHCUs							2			2
PHCU		1		1		2	2	3	2	11
PHCC				2						2
PHCC Maternity Ward	3									3
PHCC Admission Ward				2						2
PHCU/PHCC VIP Latrines		1		3		2	5	3	2	16
Public Markets						2			1	3
Livestock Markets							1		1	2
Public VIP Latrines					2	2				4
Elevated Water Tanks		1								1
Earth Roads		1			1		1		1	4
Dyke Rehabilitation									1	1
TOTALS	13	12	8	20	28	17	36	45	12	221

Source: The Republic of South Sudan, Ministry of Finance and Planning and Local Government Board, Local Governance and Service Delivery Project, July 20 to June 2016, Annual Report, Abridged Version. P. 014.

The project revised the existing PDG project designs to lower cost and integrate more contextually appropriate materials. The revisions were based on a May-June 2015 review of primary health care units (PHCU) and centres (PHCC), classroom blocks, public market units, sanitation facilities (latrines, and boreholes). All existing Payam project designs were revised and design options expanded. Altogether eleven designs were produced and adopted by respective sector ministries (Health, Education and Water).

Successful contracting processes and site handover by Counties enabled contractors to commence mobilization of materials, staff and commenced works. At the end of June 2016, 96% of the contracts had been successfully tendered and awarded and works had commenced. Only 4% of the projects [in the States of Lakes and Eastern Equatoria State (EES) did not attract bids owing to their small size relative to costs of mobilizing equipment. By the end of the financial year, efforts were underway for the remaining projects to be contracted out.[141]

b. Component 2: Community Engagement: This component continued to support the engagement of local communities in the planning, implementation and oversight of development activities at Boma, Payam and County levels. During the period under review, the project engaged communities in a total of 61 Payams of the 22 participating counties. The activities primarily involved local community mobilization and formation of Boma Development Committees (BDCs) and Payam Development Committees (PDCs); as well as conducting participatory planning and prioritization of community needs at Boma and Payam levels. A total of 333 BDCs had been established by the end of the year, with an estimated total membership of 3,088, of whom 37% are

---

141   Ibid. p. 04.

women. In the same regard, a total of 61 PDCs were established with an estimated 799 members, of whom 40% were female.

As an outcome of the community engagement, citizens feel empowered to actively participate in local government decision making by influencing and driving local development priorities through planning, monitoring and oversight of development projects. Communities also took their own initiative to contribute local resources and labour to improve existing services such as repairing broken boreholes, constructing semi permanent classrooms for children studying under trees, and clearance of community roads.

These results have been achieved with the facilitation of five NGOs contracted at the beginning of the fiscal year to implement the community engagement activities in the participating states. The activities covered under community engagement component are:[142]

i. **Conflict Sensitivity**: The project made significant steps to enhance conflict sensitivity, with PMU organizing training workshops on "conflict management and community reconciliation" at Juba; and state level in Warrap and Eastern Equatoria for project staff and FPs. The objective of the three-day events was to enhance the project's capacity for conflict awareness as well as to enhance the capacity of communities to self-mobilize and peacefully address their own conflict issues as they arise. Ultimate ownership is targeted at PDCs that are to become platforms for community reconciliation.

ii. **Grievance Redress Mechanism**: In April 2016, the project launched a mechanism that allowed communities to systematically provide feedback on the progress of project implementation. The Grievance Redress Mechanism (GRM), designed

---

142   Ibid. Pp. 05-08.

as a social accountability measure for the project, was rolled out following the completion of a pilot conducted in Western Equatoria in mid-2015. In order to achieve results, the PMU conducted training for field based project teams actively involved in the collection, management, documentation and resolution of beneficiary complaints. Overall, significant achievements were made during the fiscal year, despite delays in completing participatory planning by June 2016 as required. The shortfall is attributed to factors beyond the control of the project, notably the deteriorating macro-economic environment, insecurity and policy shifts such as the creation of 28 states which were later increased to 32 states.

c. Component 3: Institutional Strengthening: The activities carried out under this component were as follows:[143]

1. **Capacity Building**:A total of 22 Counties in seven States partici-pated and received capacity strengthening support during the fiscal year. The participating Counties were categorized as follows:

   a. The first four counties implementing Payam projects, namely: Ibba and Ezo in Western Equatoria State; Rumbek East and Yirol West in Lakes State. These counties received office equipment, furniture and power generation sets. The support packages which comprise of Starter kits were worth $30,000 each. Their officials received training through on-the-job mentoring, coaching and classroom training in thematic areas including planning, budgeting, financial management, procurement and small-scale infra-structure project implementation. At the end of the year, the counties were also assisted to prepare for audit and performance assessment.

---

143   Ibid. Pp. 09-011.

b. The second group of six counties received similar support was however not implementing Payam projects as yet. These counties received planning, budgeting and financial engagement, procurement and infrastructure projects implementation training. The counties covered were: Ikwotos and Kapoeta East in Eastern Equatoria State, Wulu in Lakes State, Gogrial West and Twic in Warrap State, and Mvolo in Western Equatoria State.

c. The third group comprised thirteen counties that were selected to participate in the project during the year. By the end of the fiscal year, they had received orientation training on county planning and budgeting. These counties were Aweil East and Aweil North in Northern Bahr el Ghazal State, Jur River and Wau in Western Bahr el Ghazal State, Yei River and Juba in Central Equatoria State, Kapoeta North and Magwi in Eastern Equatoria State; Rumbek Centre in Lakes State; Tonj North in Warrap State; and Nagero, Nzara, Maridi in Western Equatoria State.

.   A total of 296 county officers, legislative council members and contractors attended classroom training, while 355 on-the-job training (OJT) sessions were conducted.

2. **Training Materials**: The TA firm, Cowater, was tasked with the production of thematic area-specific training materials in PBFM, procurement and engineering, in the initial stage of the project. These would be used for training activities throughout the project period and beyond. The firm prepared the materials for infrastructure, procurement and PBFM training within the fiscal year. Further, five short-term technical assistance consultants were engaged to assist with the provision of specialized expertise in development of Training Guides and Review of existing

infrastructure. Consequent to the capacity building activities, counties were improving the quality of plans and budgets, and reporting better on quarterly transfers. In addition they were starting to demonstrate ability to engage communities. Overall, improvement was noted in their efficiency and effectiveness in office practice and management and keeping records.

3. **Environmental and Social Safeguards**: The issues covered under this programme were:

   a. **Training:** County and State officials were trained in Environmental and Social safeguards, during the year in all the seven states of Eastern Equatoria, Western Equatoria, Lakes, Northern Bahr el Ghazal, Western Bahr el Ghazal, Central Equatoria and Warrap. Participants from these states were drawn from various ministries and departments at state and county level. During FY 2015/16, a total of 188 personnel were trained, constituting 145 county and 43 state officials. This was an increase from FY 2014/15, when a total of 159 state and county officials were trained. Areas covered in training included education, Public Health, Physical Infrastructure, Youth, Culture and Social welfare, Agriculture and Forestry. Key training aspects included environment impact assessment, public consultation and the need for consideration of social issues in project planning and implementation. Other areas covered were: integrating environment into development planning; relevance and application of environment management tools including screening checklists, environment and social appraisal forms, environment and social monitoring and environment management planning. Environment and social screening of Payam projects was also undertaken for all the projects approved for funding-FY 2015/16.

Table 10. 3 Community Engagement: Committees and Members

Fiscal Year	State	County	No. BDCs Formed	BDC Members Trained		No. PDCs Formed	Total PDC Members Trained	
				M	F		M	F
2013/14	Lakes	Rumbek East	12	94	38	4	30	14
		Yirol East	9	76	23	3	21	12
	WES	Ezo	14	135	75	3	14	14
		Ibba	5	45	30	2	10	10
Total			40	350	166	12	75	50
2104/15	Lakes	Wulu	7	94	51	2	18	6
	WES	Mvolo	9	63	36	3	20	11
	EES	Kapoeta East	45	317	144	3	33	3
		Ikwoto	18	137	67	3	42	9
	Warrap	Twic	12	80	50	4	18	12
		Gogrial West	14	98	58	4	15	14
Total			105	789	406	18	146	55

Table 10.3 Source: The Republic of South Sudan. Ministry of Finance and Planning and Local Government Board. Local Governance and Service Delivery Project. July 20 to June 2016, Annual Report, Abridged Version. P. 015.

2015/16								
WES	Maridi	8	64	24	2	12	8	
	Nzara	8	64	24	2	14	8	
	Nagero	16	119	47	3	22	16	
	Mvolo	15	106	57	4	29	11	
Lakes	Rumbek Centre	13	85	58	3	21	12	
	Wulu	7	82	86	2	20	24	
EES	Kapoeta West	16	82	44	3	17	15	
	Kapoeta East	45	159	84	4	65	18	
	Ikwoto	17	114	62	3	36	6	
	Magwi	19	103	34	3	27	11	
Warrap	Tonj North	13	91	52	4	22	21	
	Twic	10	43	67	3	11	12	
	Gogrial West	15	60	105	5	20	29	
CES	Juba	26	215	102	6	61	35	
	Yei	9	73	23	2			
NBG	Awiel East	53	188	144	4	44	44	
	Awiel North	14	87	56	2	26	26	
WBG	Wau							
	Jur River	29	187	97	6	31	25	
Total		333	1922	1166	61	478	321	
Grand Total		478	3062	1738	91	699	426	

203

b. **Environmental and Social Safeguards Audit**: A project Environment and Social Audit was also carried out. It covered performance in the implementation of the Environment and Social Management Framework (ESMF), over the last two fiscal years, and made recommendation for improvement.

d) **Component 4: Project Management:** Activities dealt with under this programme were as the following:[144]

1. **Procurement**: Activities undertaken during the year under the sub-component included procurement of various goods and services for the PMU as well as the States. Key achievements included the recruitment of seven FPs for the seven states; construction of the perimeter fence at the Local Government Board Compound and car shed; rehabilitation of the LOGOSEED state offices in Kuajok, Torit, Wau and Aweil and rehabilitation of state office latrines in Rumbek and Yambio; and delivery of county office equipment and starter kits for the former Lakes, Eastern Equatoria, Western Equatoria and Warrap States. In addition, installation of solar systems and Internet for state offices in Torit and Kuajok was carried out. The recruitment of the State Coordinators and other staff who were 17 in total for the former Central Equatoria, Western Bahr el Ghazal and Northern Bahr el Ghazal States was done. Recruitment of three additional PMU staff who were Procurement Officer, Community Engagement Officer/Trainer and Monitoring, Reporting and Evaluation Specialist was completed.

2. **Communications**: Activities during the year included a communications campaign conducted in support of community

---

144   Ibid. P. 012

engagement in the former states in which the project was active. The campaign massages were transmitted through a three-part drama series aired over a period of three weeks in all the states. Messaging was also carried out through branded materials such as T-shirts, polo shirts and field jackets, and informational materials that included banners, wall stickers, posters and calendars. Just as was the case in FY 2014/15, the banners served as useful visual aids for the community engagement activities. The updated version of the brochure, flier, FAQ and factsheets were also produced and were disseminated in the course of FY 2016/17. The communications unit oversaw the editing, proofing and artwork and printing of the Local Government Audit and Local Government Performance Assessment manuals and strategy. The documents were launched in two separate events during the months of May and June 2015 that were well covered by the media. Further, the communications unit undertook compilation of the Quarterly Progress Reports.

3. **Monitoring and Evaluation**: A number of working sessions for state teams, state based trainers and facilitating partners to operationalize the Project Monitoring and Evaluation (PM&E) system were conducted during the year. Continuous updating of the project results framework, and continuous component specific performance analysis was also undertaken. In addition, compilation and circulation of monthly activity reports to key Project stakeholders were carried out. The Project also undertook an Annual Review and Lessons learnt workshop to promote improvement in implementation through internal learning.

4. **Financial Management**: The total financial expenditure within the period was USD 2,631,254.12 against receipts of

USD 5,251,479.86. This is considered to be a commendable achievement given the circumstances under which the project operated throughout the financial year. Generally, there has been a marked increase in transactions over the last three financial years with the highest registered during the FY 2015/16. In general, the Project's financial performance was 70% of the FY 2015/16 budget.

10.8.4. Budget for the Four Components for Local Governance and Service Delivery Project

The budget for the four components of the Local Governance and Service Delivery Project was driven from two sources: the IDA and Trust Fund. Whereas the project activities for the financial year 2015/16 was financed by IDA and the Government of Denmark. The Government of Denmark started financing the project starting at the FY 2013/14 by paying directly the salary for the Community Engagement Adviser for the project which was considered as in kind contribution.[145] The budget for the four components is as in table 10.4.

---

145   Republic of South Sudan, Ministry of Finance and Economic Planning, Local Governance and Service Delivery Project, Credit No. 51230 and TFNO. 018138. Financial Budget for the FY 2015/16, Revised August 2015. P. 1.

Table 10.4 shows the budget of the project four components:

Funding Sources	Component 1: Block Grants to Counties	Component 2: Community Engagement	Component 3: Institutional strengthening	Component 4: Project Management	Total
IDA	5,352,598	3,488,180	5,756,165	4,252,874	18,849,817
TF	2,593,664	505,720	834,535	616,586	4,550,505
Total	7,946,262	3,993,900	6,590,700	4,869,460	23,400,322

Source: Republic of South Sudan, Ministry of Finance and Economic Planning, Local Governance and Service Delivery Project, Credit No. 51230 and TFNO. 018138. Financial Budget for the FY 2015/16, Revised August 2015. P. 1.

10.8.5. Principles of Budgets for the Counties

For the Counties to prepare the budgets they should adhere to the following three key principles:[146]

1. Plans and Budgets must be realistic:

    a) The resources available to a County are limited, and the budget must be based on a realistic assessment of the resources available from:

    i. The transfers communicated by State government.

    ii. The revenues the County can collect itself.

    iii. Resources from donors.

    b) The budget must be balanced. Overall planned expenditures should not exceed the revenues the State or County expects to receive.

    c) The available revenue must be distributed across the various Departments of the County through budget ceilings. Departments must then adhere to their budget ceilings during

---

146   Op. cit. LOGOSEED Document. P. 7.

the budget preparation process so that their expenditure estimates are within their budget resource envelop.

Institutional capacity to deliver programmes should be taken into account, including constraints such as limited human resources and skills gaps. Only activities that can realistically be achieved by the agency should be budgeted for.

The time it takes to implement activities should be factored in; processes such as procurement and construction take time to complete, meaning that many activities will not be concluded within one year.

2. **Plans and Budgets must be prioritized**: Given the spending limits imposed by the budget ceilings, Departments must prioritize their planned activities very carefully. This means that budgets should not be a reflection of everything a Department would like to do, but everything that it is able to do, taking into account its limited time, human and financial resources, salary obligations and the projects that are already on-going.

3. **Plans and Budgets should quantify outputs**: Quantification of outputs wherever possible is essential for performance monitoring. For example, if the Education Department plans to undertake school inspections, the Department should set out the number of inspections it plans to make each quarter. The number actually carried out can then be compared to the planned figure.

10.8.6. Transfers to the Counties

The amounts of transfers made to the Counties for Education and service delivery units for the year 2013/14 are as in table 10.5 below. Whereas transfers made to the counties for water and health services are in tables 10.6 and 10.7 respectively. While table 10.8 entails the details of County Department Grant Allocations.

Table 10.5 shows details of Education Transfers by County:

State	County	County Education Operating Grant	County Education Capital Grant	County Transfers to Service Delivery Units
Central Equatoria	Juba	335,451	231,013	1,687,800
	Kajo-Keji	323,448	231,013	1,117,156
	Lainya	237,029	231,013	517,301
	Morobo	249,032	231,013	627,040
	Terekeka	196,220	231,013	264,608
	Yei River	301,843	231,013	1,223,592
Eastern Equatoria	Budi	237,029	231,013	692,483
	Ikotos	234,692	231,013	702,188
	Kapoeta East	181,817	231,013	196,855
	Kapoeta North	150,610	231,013	41,335
	Kapoeta South	165,013	231,013	221,180
	Lopa/Lafon	198,621	231,013	456,197
	Magwi	287,440	231,013	1,438,265
	Torit	277,838	231,013	1,115,742
Jonglei	Akobo	261,034	231,013	1,396,457
	Ayod	193,820	231,013	499,081
	Bor	263,435	231,013	1,273,534
	Duk	191,419	231,013	552,863
	Nyirol (Diror)	251,432	231,013	1,133,298
	Old Fangak	232,228	231,013	878,074
	Pibor	193,820	231,013	396,766
	Piji/Piegi	222,626	231,013	656,275
	Pochalla	174,615	231,013	430,330

	Twic East	215,424	231,013	1,394,965
	Uror (Wunror)	316,247	231,013	1,878,505
Lakes	Awerial	193,820	231,013	373,718
	Cueibet	306,644	231,013	1,134,342
	Rumbek Centre	241,830	231,013	975,402
	Rumbek East	222,626	231,013	711,604
	Rumbek North	210,623	231,013	508,900
	Wulu	198,621	231,013	412,120
	Yirol East	201,021	231,013	357,562
	Yirol West	196,220	231,013	593,011
Northern Bahr El Ghazal	Aweil Centre	253,833	231,013	1,004,670
	Aweil East	517,891	231,013	2,999,272
	Aweil North	330,650	231,013	1,399,760
	Aweil South	227,427	231,013	595,000
	Aweil West	282,639	231,013	971,162
Unity	Abiemnhom	157,812	231,013	138,086
	Guit	198,621	231,013	436,292
	Koch	227,427	231,013	730,334
	Leer	210,623	231,013	776,193
	Mayendit	217,825	231,013	897,234
	Mayom	196,220	231,013	644,304
	Panyijiar	205,822	231,013	517,252
	Rubkona	229,828	231,013	954,050
	Ruweng	220,225	231,013	569,213
Upper Nile	Akoka	150,610	231,013	102,561
	Baliet	174,615	231,013	403,636

	Fashoda	172,215	231,013	246,501
	Longchok	186,618	231,013	557,413
	Maban	184,218	231,013	432,366
	Maiwut	215,424	231,013	758,839
	Malakal	227,427	231,013	1,231,358
	Melut	165,013	231,013	256,411
	Manyo	184,218	231,013	311,349
	Nasir	297,042	231,013	1,290,339
	Panyikang	181,817	231,013	346,158
	Renk	215,424	231,013	751,428
	Ulang	234,629	231,013	882,065
Warrap	Gogrial East	253,833	231,013	742,305
	Gogrial West	354,655	231,013	1,845,597
	Tonj East	225,027	231,013	603,735
	Tonj North	301,843	231,013	1,116,621
	Tonj South	258,634	231,013	855,784
	Twic	402,665	231,013	2,478,903
Western Bahr El Ghazal	Jur River	275,438	231,013	1,010,482
	Raja	177,016	231,013	276,871
	Wau	241,830	231,013	1,075,118
Western Equatoria	Ezo	225,027	231,013	506,192
	Ibba	155,411	231,013	76,283
	Maridi	217,8825	231,013	481,453
	Mundri East	217,825	231,013	426,396
	Mundri West	215,424	231,013	411,540
	Mvolo	208,223	231,013	312,500
	Nagero	157,812	231,013	95,756
	Nzara	191,419	231,013	373,568

	Tambura	201,021	231,013	494,099
	Yambio	239,430	231,013	694,340
Total		18,250,000	18,250,000	59,939,344

Source: LOGOSEED Documents, pp. 38-40.

Table 10.6 shows the details of Water Transfers by County

State	County	Operating Grant (Salaries)	Operating Grant	Capital Grant	Total Water Grants
Central Equatoria	Juba	54,474	72,108	126,582	253,164
	Kajo-Keji	54,474	72,108	126,582	253,164
	Lainya	54,474	72,108	126,582	253,164
	Morobo	54,474	72,108	126,582	253,164
	Terekeka	54,474	72,108	126,582	253,164
	Yei	54,474	72,108	126,582	253,164
Eastern Equatoria	Budi	54,474	72,108	126,582	253,164
	Ikotos	54,474	72,108	126,582	253,164
	Kapoeta East	54,474	72,108	126,582	253,164
	Kapoeta North	54,474	72,108	126,582	253,164
	Kapoeta South	54,474	72,108	126,582	253,164
	Lopa/Lafon	54,474	72,108	126,582	253,164
	Magwi	54,474	72,108	126,582	253,164
	Torit	54,474	72,108	126,582	253,164
Jonglei	Akobo	54,474	72,108	126,582	253,164
	Ayod	54,474	72,108	126,582	253,164
	Bor South	54,474	72,108	126,582	253,164
	Duk	54,474	72,108	126,582	253,164

	Fangak	54,474	72,108	126,582	253,164
	Nyirol	54,474	72,108	126,582	253,164
	Pibor	54,474	72,108	126,582	253,164
	Piegi/Canal	54,474	72,108	126,582	253,164
	Pochalla	54,474	72,108	126,582	253,164
	Twic East	54,474	72,108	126,582	253,164
	Uror	54,474	72,108	126,582	253,164
Lakes	Awerial	54,474	72,108	126,582	253,164
	Cueibet	54,474	72,108	126,582	253,164
	Rumbek Centre	54,474	72,108	126,582	253,164
	Rumbek East	54,474	72,108	126,582	253,164
	Rumbek North	54,474	72,108	126,582	253,164
	Wulu	54,474	72,108	126,582	253,164
	Yirol East	54,474	72,108	126,582	253,164
	Yirol West	54,474	72,108	126,582	253,164
Northern Bahr El Ghazal	Aweil Centre	54,474	72,108	126,582	253,164
	Aweil East	54,474	72,108	126,582	253,164
	Aweil North	54,474	72,108	126,582	253,164
	Aweil South	54,474	72,108	126,582	253,164
	Aweil West	54,474	72,108	126,582	253,164
Unity	Abiemnhom	54,474	72,108	126,582	253,164
	Guit	54,474	72,108	126,582	253,164
	Koch	54,474	72,108	126,582	253,164
	Leer	54,474	72,108	126,582	253,164
	Mayendit	54,474	72,108	126,582	253,164
	Mayom	54,474	72,108	126,582	253,164
	Pariang	54,474	72,108	126,582	253,164
	Panyijar	54,474	72,108	126,582	253,164

	Rubkona	54,474	72,108	126,582	253,164
Upper Nile	Akoka	54,474	72,108	126,582	253,164
	Baliet	54,474	72,108	126,582	253,164
	Fashoda	54,474	72,108	126,582	253,164
	Longchok	54,474	72,108	126,582	253,164
	Luakping/ Nasir	54,474	72,108	126,582	253,164
	Maban	54,474	72,108	126,582	253,164
	Maiwut	54,474	72,108	126,582	253,164
	Malakal	54,474	72,108	126,582	253,164
	Manyo	54,474	72,108	126,582	253,164
	Melut	54,474	72,108	126,582	253,164
	Panyikang	54,474	72,108	126,582	253,164
	Renk	54,474	72,108	126,582	253,164
	Ulang	54,474	72,108	126,582	253,164
Warrap	Gogrial East	54,474	72,108	126,582	253,164
	Gogrial West	54,474	72,108	126,582	253,164
	Tonj East	54,474	72,108	126,582	253,164
	Tonj North	54,474	72,108	126,582	253,164
	Tonj South	54,474	72,108	126,582	253,164
	Twic	54,474	72,108	126,582	253,164
Western Bahr El Ghazal	Jur River	54,474	72,108	126,582	253,164
	Raja	54,474	72,108	126,582	253,164
	Wau	54,474	72,108	126,582	253,164
Western Equatoria	Ezo	54,474	72,108	126,582	253,164
	Ibba	54,474	72,108	126,582	253,164
	Maridi	54,474	72,108	126,582	253,164
	Mundri East	54,474	72,108	126,582	253,164
	Mundri West	54,474	72,108	126,582	253,164

	Mvolo	54,474	72,108	126,582	253,164
	Nagero	54,474	72,108	126,582	253,164
	Nzara	54,474	72,108	126,582	253,164
	Tambura	54,474	72,108	126,582	253,164
	Yambio	54,474	72,108	126,582	253,164
Total		4,303,446	5,696,532	9,999,978	19,999,956

Source: LOGOSEED Documents, p. 41-43.

Table 10.7 Shows Details of Health Transfers by County

State	County	CHD Operating Grant	CHD Operating Grant	Total CHD Grants
Central Equatoria	Juba	514,892	253,165	768,056
	Kajo-Keji	343,352	253,165	596,517
	Lainya	238,955	253,165	492,119
	Morobo	252,881	253,165	506,046
	Terekeka	288,743	253,165	541,908
	Yei	348,246	253,165	601,411
Eastern Equatoria	Budi	248,589	253,165	501,753
	Ikotos	234,407	253,165	487,571
	Kapoeta East	311,748	253,165	564,912
	Kapoeta North	252,375	253,165	505,540
	Kapoeta South	229,359	253,165	482,523
	Lopa/Lafon	255,374	253,165	508,539
	Magwi	317,429	253,165	570,594
	Torit	249,116	253,165	502,280
Jonglei	Akobo	284,663	253,165	537,828
	Ayod	287,658	253,165	540,822
	Bor South	367,412	253,165	620,577
	Duk	215,828	253,165	468,992
	Fangak	259,243	253,165	512,408
	Nyirol	257,824	253,165	510,988
	Pibor	296,618	253,165	549,783
	Piegi/Canal	248,461	253,165	501,625
	Pochalla	216,425	253,165	469,590
	Twic East	235,089	253,165	488,253
	Uror	325,902	253,165	579,067

Lakes	Awerial	197,750	253,165	450,914
	Cueibet	266,675	253,165	519,840
	Rumbek Centre	301,565	253,165	554,729
	Rumbek East	271,624	253,165	524,788
	Rumbek North	194,211	253,165	447,375
	Wulu	191,423	253,165	444,588
	Yirol East	217,596	253,165	470,760
	Yirol West	252,479	253,165	505,643
Northern Bahr El Ghazal	Aweil Centre	192,668	253,165	445,832
	Aweil East	453,980	253,165	707,145
	Aweil North	277,760	253,165	530,924
	Aweil South	223,838	253,165	477,002
	Aweil West	313,911	253,165	567,076
Unity	Abiemnhom	168,480	253,165	421,645
	Guit	184,068	253,165	437,232
	Koch	224,868	253,165	478,033
	Leer	203,580	253,165	456,744
	Mayendit	204,321	253,165	457,486
	Mayom	269,560	253,165	522,725
	Pariang	232,256	253,165	485,421
	Panyijiar	201,339	253,165	454,503
	Rubkona	249,599	253,165	502,764
Upper Nile	Akoka	167,799	253,165	420,964
	Baliet	182,794	253,165	435,959
	Fashoda	187,493	253,165	440,658
	Longochuk	213,467	253,165	466,632
	Luakpiny/ Nasir	356,589	253,165	609,753

	Maban	195,992	253,165	449,157
	Maiwut	229,351	253,165	482,515
	Malakal	275,182	253,165	528,347
	Manyo	188,947	253,165	442,112
	Melut	199,895	253,165	453,060
	Panyikang	196,177	253,165	449,341
	Renk	286,165	253,165	539,330
	Ulang	234,792	253,165	487,956
Warrap	Gogrial East	252,569	253,165	505,734
	Gogrial West	389,650	253,165	642,814
	Tonj East	265,083	253,165	518,248
	Tonj North	312,942	253,165	566,106
	Tonj South	236,300	253,165	489,465
	Twic	351,621	253,165	604,785
Western Bahr El Ghazal	Jur River	276,438	253,165	529,602
	Raga	204,864	253,165	458,029
	Wau	299,391	253,165	552,556
Western Equatoria	Ezo	230,714	253,165	483,879
	Ibba	192,709	253,165	445,873
	Maridi	232,274	253,165	485,438
	Mundri East	198,995	253,165	452,159
	Mundri West	185,014	253,165	438,179
	Mvolo	198,815	253,165	451,980
	Nagero	161,721	253,165	414,885
	Nzara	215,949	253,165	469,113
	Tambura	205,863	253,165	459,028
	Yambio	300,304	253,165	553,469
Total	79	20,000,000	20,000,000	40,000,000

Source: LOGOSEED Documents, p. 44-46.

Table 10.8 Shows Details of County Development Grant (CDG) Allocations

State	County	County Block Grant	County Development Grant
Central Equatoria	Juba	1,287,229	6,547,827
	Kajo-Keji	858,381	3,453,524
	Lainya	597,386	1,570,351
	Morobo	632,203	1,821,565
	Terekeka	721,859	2,468,466
	Yei	870,616	3,541,804
Sub-Total	6	4,967,674	19,403,537
Eastern Equatoria	Budi	621,471	1,744,133
	Ikotos	586,016	1,488,313
	Kapoeta East	779,369	2,883,422
	Kapoeta North	630,938	1,812,440
	Kapoeta South	573,396	1,397,255
	Lopa/Lafon	638,436	1,866,540
	Magwi	793,573	2,985,909
	Torit	622,790	1,753,645
Sub-Total	8	5,245,990	15,931,657
Jonglei	Akobo	711,658	2,394,867
	Ayod	719,144	2,448,879
	Bor South	918,530	3,887,522
	Duk	539,569	1,153,179
	Fangak	648,108	1,936,324
	Nyirol	644,560	1,910,724
	Pibor	741,545	2,610,512
	Piegi/Canal	621,152	1,741,830

	Pochalla	541,063	1,163,957
	Twic East	587,722	1,500,620
	Uror	814,755	3,138,751
Sub-Total	11	7,487,807	23,887,164
Lakes	Awerial	494,375	827,083
	Cueibet	666,688	2,070,388
	Rumbek Centre	753,912	2,699,741
	Rumbek East	679,059	2,159,652
	Rumbek North	485,527	763,242
	Wulu	478,558	712,957
	Yirol East	543,990	1,185,073
	Yirol West	631,196	1,814,304
Sub-Total	8	4,733,304	12,232,440
Northern Bahr El Ghazal	Aweil Centre	481,669	735,409
	Aweil East	1,134,951	5,449,082
	Aweil North	694,399	2,270,332
	Aweil South	559,595	1,297,669
	Aweil West	784,778	2,922,455
Sub-Total	5	3,655,392	12,674,948
Unity	Abiemnom	421,201	299,108
	Guit	460,170	580,282
	Koch	562,170	1,316,254
	Leer	508,949	932,242
	Mayendit	510,803	945,622
	Mayom	673,901	2,122,431
	Pariang	580,641	1,449,526
	Panyijar	503,347	891,820
	Rubkona	623,998	1,762,366
Sub-Total	9	4,845,180	10,299,650
Upper Nile	Akoka	419,498	286,818

	Baliet	456,985	557,302
	Fashoda	468,733	642,065
	Longochuk	533,667	1,110,595
	Luakpiny/Nasir	891,472	3,692,290
	Maban	489,981	795,382
	Maiwut	573,377	1,397,114
	Malakal	687,956	2,223,845
	Manyo	472,368	668,298
	Melut	499,738	865,781
	Panyikang	490,442	798,705
	Renk	715,413	2,421,961
	Ulang	586,979	1,495,258
Sub-Total	13	7,286,609	16,955,414
Warrap	Gogrial East	631,423	1,815,939
	Gogrial West	974,125	4,288,659
	Tonj East	662,709	2,042,676
	Tonj North	782,354	2,904,960
	Tonj South	590,751	1,522,475
	Twic	879,052	3,602,674
Sub-Total	6	4,520,413	16,176383
Western Bahr El Ghazal	Jur River	691,095	2,246,491
	Raga	512,161	955,415
	Wau	748,478	2,660,533
Sub-Total	3	4,520,413	16,176,383
Western Equatoria	Ezo	576,786	1,421,711
	Ibba	481,772	736,148
	Maridi	580,685	1,449,843
	Mundri East	497,486	849,535
	Mundri West	462,536	597,354

	Mvolo	497,038	846,300
	Nagero	404,302	177,175
	Nzara	539,871	1,155,359
	Tambura	514,658	973,437
	Yambio	750,761	2,677,008
Sub-Total	10	5,305,896	10,883,870
Grand Total	79	50,000,000	144,307,500

Source: LOGOSEED Documents, Pp. 47-50.

10.8.7. Local Government Audit and Performance Assessment

Beneficiary assessment of the LOGOSEED project was done in November 2018. After the results of the assessment, the following recommendations were made:[147]

10.8.7.1. Project Management Level

a. **Changes to fit the current administrative divisions within GRSS**: For future projects, the changes in the administrative local government structures must be followed and efforts made to ensure that such changes do not affect implementation at all. One of the approaches is to apply for a waiver on staff transfers in counties of focus to allow for proper continuous capacity development efforts to take root.

b. **Develop and Implement exit strategies well in time**: In future, the exit strategies must be applied at least one year to the end to ensure that all beneficiaries are adequately prepared where the project exists.

c. **A fast-track plan for the remaining Sub-projects**: A plan to ensure that all uncompleted projects are finished within the

---

147   Republic of South Sudan, LOGOSEED. Beneficiary Assessment of the Local Government and Service Delivery Project (LGSDP)-ID-127079, Final Report, November 2018. P. 75-77.

remaining time is needed. A clear plan that indicates the amount of work, the time required for quality to be guaranteed and the payment to be made should be done and managed exquisitely.

d. **Improve Results-Based M&E:** In future projects, a fully pledged M&E framework should be designed and implemented from the initiation of the project, through tracking key baseline indicators and developing data capture tools for annual reporting towards impact and outcomes. The M&E system should have a dashboard that presents periodic performance trends of the project at indicator level, that facilitate decision making on what needs to be done to achieve the project goal.

e. **Tracking the Ripple Effect**: The M&E system should be able to track the project's ripple effect and impact in employing people, buying local materials and the value of community contribution in future. SMART[148] indicators at output and impact level for every component should be developed to ensure comprehensive monitoring and reporting.

10.8.7.2. Implementation Level

a. **Building sustainable internal mechanisms for institutional development**: Although the trained staff reported having trained others under the institutional development component, the results would have been better if a more structured internal arrangement was made. For the future, it may be better to have an arrangement for training of trainers (ToTs) who would ensure in-house capacity building for other staff in a more structured and supervised way.

b. **Capacity building for PDC members in project monitoring and quality assurance**: In the future designs, tailor-made

---

148   Specific, Measureable, Attainable, Realistic and Time bound are key ingredients of an indicator.

training for PDC members, PSTs and PMTs should be done to foster quality control. The idea is to empower the community structures with more detailed knowledge of specific sub-projects, to ensure better quality monitoring and approval processes. For example, PDCs can be given basic skills in monitoring road project construction.

c. **Training of hand pump mechanics in new technologies**: There is a need to offer refresher training to all hand pump mechanics in the use of the latest technologies for boreholes. This can be done under the auspices of county institutional development, given the role the hand pump mechanics play in ensuring the sustainability of water projects.

d. **The localization of Starter kits especially electronics**: In future, where starter kits are considered, localization of these to the needs of a country should be made. In simple terms, a printer that is purchased for Jur River County should be one that has spare parts and technicians available in Jur River County. The same applies to motorcycles and any other items that need a local context.

e. **Improved Communication between PMU and counties**: There is a need for improved communication between the PMU and the counties; one that ensures periodic updates on critical decisions and offers feedback that is bottom up and vice versa. Communication would include dissemination of key findings of studies, audits that allows the County-level officials to give feedback, get responses and foster learning and development through such interactive platforms.

f. **Support PDC and County administration relationships**: In the future projects, the sustainability of PDCs should be hinged on the County administration for support supervision and consultations. With formal recognition of their role, and involvement in County and Payam level planning and development activities, the PDCs' sustainability would be enhanced.

g. **Encourage and promote the transition of the PSTs and PMTs into user committees**: The PSTs and PMTs would be very valuable members of the user committee because of the substantial knowledge of the physical conditions and construction dynamics of the sub-projects. The transition from PSTs to user committees should be promoted in the future, for purposes of improving sustainability even though it reduces on the number of community members that participate in the various sub-structures.

h. **A more structured real-time response mechanisms on grievances**: There is need to have a more structured and real-time response mechanism to the various grievances raised at least at the PMU level, where each grievance raised should be followed by a meeting to address the grievances with a clear course of action communicated on time. In the same way, a follow-up mechanism of complaints raised at the country level can be implemented by the PMU through the state coordination office, to ensure real-time feedback to the beneficiaries. It would be advisable to establish a third party who collects grievances and forwards them to the rightful offices, as well as follows up their response actions. This third party should not be a member of the FPs, counties or PMU since some of the grievances are related to their performance and conduct.

10.9. Local Government Services Rendered by German Development Cooperation (GIZ)

10.9.1. Introduction

After decades of civil war, South Sudan declared its independence in 2011 and became the world's youngest sovereign state. However, the hope harboured by its citizens for a peaceful future and growing prosperity has not yet been realized. Within South Sudan, armed conflict resumed again in December 2013.

As one of the world's most fragile states, South Sudan faces numerous challenges, including a lack of capacity to deliver basic public services, the absence of state monopoly on the use of force, inadequate legitimacy, and extremely limited development prospects. In all, a large part of the population in South Sudan have become internally displaced persons, many of whom have fled to urban areas in search for provision of services, as well as income generating opportunities.

This means that a disproportionately large number of people were reliant on the services provided by the urban administrations. Compared with rural regions, towns and cities offer fewer opportunities for subsistence farming as a means of securing livelihoods, such as the lack of necessary resources and capacities needed to overcome structural changes, especially if external shocks occur at the same time (e.g. as a result of violent conflicts, epidemics, droughts or floods).

Inadequate resilience in urban areas is the core problem to be addressed by the GIZ Programme of Strengthening Local Governance and Resilience in South Sudan since 2007.

10.9.2. Objective of the GIZ Programme

The main objective of the GIZ Programme is: The resilience of urban areas is strengthened.[149]

10.9.3. Fields of Action

The programme was designed to boost the resilience of the urban areas in three fields of action[150] which are as below.

10.9.3.1. Strengthening the Capacity to Deliver Services in Urban Administrations

The aim of this field of action was to strengthen the capacities and develop methods in local administrations for the delivery of public services, for example in the areas of water and sanitation, waste and energy, or for the operation of markets or slaughter houses.

The activities of this field of action were as follows:

1. Implement governance models.
2. Realize a course on governance models.
3. Organize a flat form for urban administrations.
4. Define the roles of responsibilities of urban administrations.
5. Establish a network of women in managerial positions within the urban administrations, city councils and traditional authorities.

10.9.3.2. Improving the Capacities of Urban Administrations to Respond to External Shocks

The aim of this field of action was to place local authorities in a position to proactively tackle possible external shocks so as to minimize their negative impacts on the population. The activities of this field of action included the following:

---

149   German Cooperation, Strengthening Local Governance and Resilience in South Sudan, Programme Outline 2016-2017.
150   Ibid.

1. Realize contingency management courses.
2. Create contingency plans.
3. Implement contingency plans.

10.9.3.3. Improving Participation by the Civil Society in the Political and Administrative Work of the Urban Administrations

The aim of this field of action was to strengthen participation in the urban authorities' political and administrative work by the most diverse social actors. To this end, the programme focused on two sub-areas:

i.   Available information (local and national) as a prerequisite for solid decision-making; and
ii. Local dialogue between local authorities and residents, including the creation of concrete feedback mechanisms.

The activities of this field of action covered the following:
1. Establish participation mechanisms.
2. Explain the newly created administrative structure to citizens.
3. Utilize the Knowledge Management Information System (KMIS).

The summary of the programmes implemented by GIZ from 2007 to 2017 are as in table 10.9 below.

Table 10.9 shows summary of the programmes implemented by GIZ from 2007 to 2017

Year	Programmes Implemented
05/2007-12/2010	1. Support for Administration Reform & Decentralization in Southern Sudan. 2. Improving the Conditions for decentralized Public Administration.
01/2011-12/2013	3. Support for Administration Reform & Decentralization in Southern Sudan. 4. Supporting Structural Change Processes, Rule of Law Structures and Good (Financial) Governance.
01/2014-12/2015	5. Decentralization and Accountability in South Sudan. 6. Supporting Peace and Dialogue-Promoting Initiatives in View of the Domestic Political and Humanitarian Crisis.
01/2016-12/2017	7. Strengthening Local Governance & Resilience in South Sudan. 8. Improving Capacities for Service Delivery and Contingency Planning at Local Level.

Source: German Cooperation, Strengthening Local Governance and Resilience in South Sudan, Programme Outline 2016-2017.

10.9.3.4. Support of GIZ for Water and Sanitation Services in Equatoria Region–South Sudan

GIZ has also given support for the establishment of Yei Town Water and Sanitation Services Ltd. (YTWSS); Yambio Urban Water and Sanitation Services Company Ltd. (YUWASO); and Torit Urban Water Supply and sanitation Services Ltd. (TUWSS).

10.9.3.5. GIZ Support to Yei Water and Sanitation Services Ltd. (YTWSS)

YTWSS has been supported by GIZ since its establishment in 2012. Besides customized advisory services to improve management and operations, GIZ has provided financial subsidies to ensure operational cost coverage as well as water supply infrastructure, equipment and spare parts. Comprehensive capacity development measures, including training and coaching of utility staff that have been implemented. Additionally, GIZ has assisted in preparing a business plan as well as establishment and introduction of sustainable and affordable tariff system.[151]

10.9.3.6. GIZ Support to Yambio Urban Water and Sanitation Services Company Ltd, (YUWASO)

YUWASO has been supported by GIZ since its establishment in 2013. Besides customized advisory services to improve management and operations, GIZ has provided financial subsidies to ensure operational cost coverage as well as water supply infrastructure, equipment and spare parts. Comprehensive capacity development measures, including training and coaching of utility staff, have been implemented. Additionally, GIZ has assisted in preparing a business plan as well as establishing and introducing a sustainable and affordable tariff system.[152]

---

151   German Cooperation, FACTSHEET, Yei Town Water and Sanitation Services Ltd. (YTWSS).
152   German Cooperation, FACTSHEET, Yambio Urban Water and Sanitation Services Company Ltd. (YUWASO).

10.9.3.7. GIZ Support to Torit Urban Water Supply and Sanitation Services Ltd. (TUWSS)

TUWSS has been supported by GIZ since its establishment in 2015. Besides customized advisory services to improve management and operations, GIZ has provided financial subsidies to ensure operational cost as well as rehabilitation of the office building, provision of office, IT equipment and spare parts. Comprehensive capacity development measures, including training and coaching of utility staff, have been implemented. Additionally, GIZ has assisted in establishing and introducing a sustainable and affordable tariff system.[153]

10.9.3.8. GIZ Support to Training of Local Government Officers

GIZ has been involved in the programme for training of Local Government Officers (LGOs). Training programme was started in 2019. Five training of trainers (ToTs) for local government officers were implemented. 99 LGOs were selected from the states of the three regions of Bahr el Ghazal, Equatoria and Upper Nile and trained to train LGOs. LGOs were trained in Wau, Juba and Malakal. LGOs trained in Wau were 33, Juba 27, and Malakal 39 respectively.[154]

---

153   German Cooperation, FACTSHEET, Torit Urban Water Supply and Sanitation Services Ltd. (TUWSS).

154   Interview with Del Rumdit Deng, Executive Secretary, Local Government Board.

CHAPTER ELEVEN

TONJ SOUTH COUNTY AND TONJ MUNICIPALITY AS SPECIAL CASES FOR THE STUDY

11.1. Introduction

Tonj South County and Tonj Municipality were selected among the counties and municipalities in South Sudan as models to represent other counties and municipalities for both of them are located within Tonj Town.

11.2. Establishment of Tonj South County

Tonj South County was established in 2004 by the SPLM/A as one of the institutions of Civil Authority of New Sudan (CANS). Before 2004 it was part of Thiet Rural Council within Tonj Area Council.

When Tonj State was created in 2006, proper/legal procedures were not considered, only accommodation of politicians was given importance. The State Authorities quickly declared Tonj Town as a

Municipality. The area of the municipality covers seven miles radius from the centre of the town. There was no survey made to determine the number of block and quarter councils. Appointments were made without survey. It became apparent that Tonj Municipality had no areas to administer. The Bomas surrounding Tonj Town belonged to Tonj South County.

11.3. Departments of Tonj South County
Tonj South County had a Municipality which was a separate entity with an independent administration, and seven Payams.[155] The Payams were: Tonj, Manyangok, Yar, Wanhalel, Thiet, Jak and Agugo. It also has twenty one Bomas.

The departments under Tonj South County were as follows:
1. Education;
2. Health;
3. Rural Development;
4. Agriculture;
5. Social Welfare; and
6. Lands.

11.4. Services being rendered by Tonj South County
Some departments of the County are rendering services to the population of the County. For example, health, education, water, police, fire brigade and agriculture services are being provided by the County Administration. These departments are in principle County Departments but practically they are accountable to their respective ministries at the State level or at the national level.

The Ministry of Agriculture had made an initiative to encourage farming and people embarked in cultivating food crops.

155   Interview with Mr. Marko Mabior Ajiec, Executive Director, Tonj South County.

11.5. Sources of Revenue of Tonj South County

The sources of revenue for Tonj South County are as follows:

1. Social Service Tax.
2. Court Fees and Fines.
3. Market Fees.
4. Local Imports and Export Produce Tax.
5. Auction Fees (cows and goats).
6. Land Fees.
7. Permits.
8. Royalties.
9. Butchery Fees.
10. Bridges Fees.
11. Grants from the National Ministry of Finance and Planning.

It is apparent that not all the sources of revenue stated in the Constitution and Local Government Act, 2009 are being collected by the counties. That in itself is a deviation from the national statutes.

Before the formation of the State Revenue Authority (SRA), the County was getting the revenue from the above mentioned sources and the collection of revenues was very good. The County was retaining 60% of the revenues and 40% of the revenues was remitted to the State Treasury. When the State Revenue Authority (SRA) was established in 2018/19, after that, the collection did not go on well. There became a multiple number of courts and consequently did not function well for they had jurisdiction on the same subjects.

11.6. Grants from the National Government for Tonj South County

The County gets grants from the National Ministry of Finance through the State Ministry of Finance to meet the salaries of the employees but there are no any allocations for operation cost.

11.7. Role of Tonj South County Council

Tonj South County has a Council. Members were selected to the County Council. The appointment of the council members was done through communities' consultation.[156]

The roles of Tonj South County Council are:

1. It is the watchdog of the executive.
2. It promulgates laws and oversees the management of the resources of the County.
3. It ascertains that, development projects are initiated by writing project proposals, and to ascertain that the projects are financed and implemented.
4. It is the responsibility of the Council to influence the communities that fall within the jurisdiction of Tonj South County to initiate stability to live in peace and unity.

At the onset of the Council there was resentment from the County Authorities. They delayed swearing in of the members of the Council for the fear of the Commissioner to be impeached or may restrict the Commissioner from taking unilateral decisions. But later on these issues were addressed and members were allowed to take oath.

Another role played by the Council is the drafting of bills. Some bills have been drafted but not tabled to the Council for

---

156   Interview with Mr. Marko Mabior Ajiec, Executive Director, Tonj South County.

promulgation. This is due to the lack of funds for the development of bills. The Council is a voluntary legislature for there is no sitting allowance, and the Council is supposed to sit twice in a month. In a nutshell, the relationship between the Commissioner and the Council was cordial.[157]

11.8. Tonj Municipality
11.8.1. Creation of Tonj Municipality
Tonj Municipality was created in 2016 by Hon. Akec Tonj Aleu, the First Governor of Tonj State[158] when Warrap State got splitted into three states namely: Tonj, Gogrial and Twic. At that time, Tonj Town became the capital town of Tonj State and its status was raised to that of municipality. The jurisdiction of Tonj Municipality falls within seven miles radius from the centre of Tonj Town.

In 2016, at the inception of Tonj Municipality, Joseph Anei Mador was appointed as the First Mayor of Tonj Municipality and Kiir Mangong was elected by the appointed members of Tonj Municipality Council, as the Chairman of Tonj Municipal Council. Members of the Council were selected by consultation with their communities. Municipal jurisdiction authority operated within seven miles radius of the town, whereas Tonj South County jurisdiction administration operates beyond seven miles from the jurisdiction of the Municipality[159] but both had their headquarters in Tonj Town.

Tonj Municipality was by then "divided into six blocks, namely: Deng Nhial, Genanyuon, Wunalel, Kalkuel, Wargiir and Makuei. Each block was in turn divided into quarters. However,

157 Interview with Hon. Gabriel Majok Manyual, Chairman of Tonj County Council.
158 Interview with Mr. Natale Nhial Deng, Chief Executive Officer, Tonj Municipality.
159 Interview with Natale Nhial Deng.

there came to be a conflict between Tonj South County and Tonj Municipality Administrations over the areas of jurisdiction. The Municipality on one hand claimed people who are residents of Makuei and Wargiir Blocks for they fall within the seven miles radius of the Municipality, whereas on the other hand Tonj South County claimed the same blocks to fall within the Payams under its jurisdiction."[160] With this situation, "Tonj Municipality had four blocks and ten quarters. The blocks and quarters were administered by Grade 10 Local Government Administrative Officers."[161] The conflict over the jurisdictions between Tonj South County and Tonj Municipality were not resolved until the revocation of the 32 states which abolished the instituted institutions of the 32 states and reverted to the institutions of the past 10 states.

11.8.2. Services Rendered
Tonj Municipality rendered some services to the residents of the town. For example, health and education services were provided as well as water services. Local roads in the town were maintained and Tonj Town was surveyed.

11.8.3. Sources of Revenue of Tonj Municipality
From the six blocks of Tonj Municipality, the Municipality operated in four blocks namely: Deng Nhial, Wanhalel, Genanyuon and Kalkuel. The other two blocks: Makuei and Wargiir did not have any effective administration under the Municipality for they were zones of conflict between the Municipality and Tonj South County. Because of the claim by Tonj South County that these two blocks fall within their jurisdiction, and more over Makuei is a territory

---

160   Interview with Diing Aleu Diing, Inspector of Local Government, Tonj Municipality.
161   Interview with Natale Nhial Deng.

under Manyangok County, the Governor by then gave an order to let Makuei be reverted back to Manyangok County. Whereas the issue of Wargiir was also suspended by the Governor until in the future when the issue of the boundaries has to be determined by the boundaries dispute committee. Kuanyja Block was a new block added to fall under the administration of Tonj Municipality and effectively functioned well under Tonj Municipal administration.[162]

Before the establishment of the State Revenue Authority (SRA), the main sources of revenue for Tonj Municipality were as the following:

1. Social Service Tax
2. Households Tax.
3. Tonj Bridges fees.
4. Main Market fees.
5. Malith Market (Manyata) fees.
6. Cows Auction fees.
7. Wau and Thiet Parks fees.
8. Block Councils' Courts fees and fines.
9. Check Point Parking fees.
10. Land fees.
11. Goat Auction fees.

After the establishment of the SRA, some of the sources of Tonj Municipality revenue were taken over by SRA and the Municipality was left with the following as sources of revenue:

1. Cows Auction fees.
2. Block Councils Court fees and fines.
3. Ten Percent from Check Point Parking fees.
4. Households Tax within the surveyed areas in the town.

---

162   Interview with Mr. Diing Aleu Diing, Inspector of Local Government, Tonj Municipality.

11.8.4. Departments of Tonj Municipality

Tonj Municipality had the following departments as stipulated in
the Municipality's By-Laws of 2017:

1. General Administration.
2. Finance and Economic Development.
3. Agriculture, Forestry and City Beautification.
4. Planning, Budget and Project Management.
5. Directorate of Hygiene and Sanitation.
6. Directorate of Engineering and Public Works.
7. Directorate of Information Technology and Establishment.
8. Directorate of Public Order

Despite the existence of these Tonj Municipality departments,
their achievements were not explicit.

11.8.5. Grants for Tonj Municipality

Grants from the National Government for Tonj Municipality were
channeled through the State. The personnel of the Municipality
were paid salaries by the State Government; and sum of SSP7,000
was paid monthly as operational cost which was an insignificant
amount to suffice the needs of the Municipality. Whereas in the
budget the allocated amount was SSP21,000, and there was no any
allocation for capital. Even the allocated amount as operational cost
is insignificant to cater for any services that could have an impact in
provision of services and change the livelihood of the population
in Tonj Municipality.

11.8.6. Achievements of Tonj Municipality

However, with these meager resources, the Municipality was able to
carry out some developmental structures. A building to house the

office of the Chairman of Tonj Municipal Council and the Council Meetings Hall was constructed. Apart from that, some office furnitures such as tables and chairs were procured as well as fuel for emergency operations. Moreover, the Municipality constructed two junctions in Tonj Town which were: Tonj-Thiet Road and Tonj-Wau Road.

On the other hand, Tonj Municipality By-Laws 2017 were passed by the Council and assented to by the Council Chairperson and the Mayor. This law although it was in place, there was no ad herence to it. The purpose of the by-laws was to regulate the works of Tonj Municipality and provide penalties which govern the criminal acts or violation of the provisions of by-laws or local orders that may be adjudicated upon by the courts, and other issues related thereto.[163]

11.8.7. Tonj Municipal Council

Since its establishment in 2017, Tonj Municipal Council has not been playing any effective role after they had passed the By-Laws. There was a difference between the Councillors and the Mayor. The Councillors used to defend their areas and they were not being paid allowances, this had consequently had a negative impact and resulted to the abstinence of the Councillors from their duties.

The job of the Chairman of the Council had been made to be a part-time business, whereas the law stipulates that it is a full-time job but the Chairman doesn't come to the office.

The members of the Council were temporarily engaged pending elections to be conducted.

---

163   Tonj State, Tonj Municipality By-Laws, 2017. P.4.

CHAPTER TWELVE

AN EVALUATION OF LOCAL GOVERNMENT ADMINISTRATION IN SOUTH SUDAN

12.1. Summary

Local Government Act, 2009 was promulgated before South Sudan could attain its independence on 9 July 2011, and therefore it still carries the title of Southern Sudan.

The objectives, principles, criteria for creation of local government councils as corporate bodies and organs of the councils, responsibilities of the councils have been well articulated in the Local Government Act, 2009. The functions of the Executive Council, powers and functions of the commissioner and mayor are also clearly articulated. However, all the provisions of Local

Government Act, 2009 have not been followed accurately. There is lack behind in the implementation of the Local Government Act, 2009. For example, even if the councils are nominated by their constituencies, they are not involved in decision making. It is either the state governments or the commissioners who take unilateral decisions without consultation with the councilors. The departments established in the counties are mostly accountable to their states' departments and do not provide adequate services to the grass roots. Warrants for the establishment of local councils whether at County or Payam levels have not been issued.

Some parts of the criteria for the establishment of a county are not fulfilled as prescribed by the LGA 2009, for example, the size of the population; and economic viability of 35%-45% of total annual budget. It is the same with the city council e.g. Juba City Council does not fulfill the economic viability of 75%-100% of the total annual budget; as well as the Quarter Councils population of 20,000-25,000 is not ad hered to when creating a quarter council in the towns. Moreover, the Municipal Council fall below the prescribed size of population of 100,000-300,000 people, e.g. Wau Municipality which falls within Western Bahr el Ghazal State does not fulfill this situation. It is the population of the whole state which is about 333,000 according to the 2008 Population Census. Economic viability of 63%-75% of the total annual budget is not met by municipalities. Town councils do not meet the criteria of the size of population of 50,000-100,000; and economic viability of 55%-65% of total annual budget.

The organs of the councils (legislature, executive and customary law) exist by name in the LGA 2009 but are not operational even if they are formed. The councils are not exercising the responsibilities prescribed in the LGA 2009.

No services being rendered by the local government councils. Some NGOs e.g. UNDP, UNICEF, Oxfam, CEPO, GIZ, World Vision, CCM and others render some services in the fields of health, agriculture, relief, water and education.

Local councils do not collect much revenue from sources of revenue generation besides Social Service Tax, Court Fees and Fines, market fees and auction fees. Councils depend much on grant-in-aid from the national government.

Another criteria not fulfilled is that for the establishment of the Executive Chieftainship. There are a number of executive chieftainships established without observing the set criteria and this has brought up a multiple of chieftainships which have brought confusion among the chiefs, and the chiefs are not able to remit the required amount of social service tax they are supposed to pay to the councils.

Although the Local Government Board is trying its best to promote the well being of local government institutions in the country, the fact that its functions and powers are limited to review and formulation of local government policies as well as recommendation and coordination of the establishment of minimum standards and uniform norms for service delivery makes it not much effective in enforcing the implementation of the Local Government Act in letter and spirit.

It is explicit that in South Sudan there is no conviction to law, and it is what is making the implementation of Local Government Act to be disregarded by the national and states' leaderships, which brought the failure of both governments to provide adequate service delivery to the rural populace. Rather, it is the donors and partners who have played much role in supporting local government for provision of basic services.

The evaluation of local government administration in South Sudan is concluded with narration of its challenges and recommendations of prospects for its progress as provided in 12.2 and 12.3 below.

12.2. Challenges Facing Local Government Administration in South Sudan

The challenges facing local government administration of South Sudan are as hereunder:

1. **Diversity of local governance**: The quality of local governance in South Sudan is highly heterogeneous as a result of diverse historical, cultural and ethnic characteristics, additionally complicated by decades of conflict and social dislocation. Moreover, the nature of ethnic and clan based social organization and the role of traditional authorities varies widely across South Sudan's regions.

2. **Formal   local   government   structure**: The   2005 Comprehensive Peace Agreement and the Interim Constitution of South Sudan (ICSS), 2005 laid out a 'democratic decentralized system of government'. This was detailed in the 2009 Local Government Act (LGA), and retained after independence in the 2011 Transitional Constitution. The system comprises national, state and local governments. Local government is subdivided into Counties, Payams and Bomas in the rural areas; and into City/Municipal Councils, Town Councils, Block and Quarter Councils in the urban areas. Provisions for public participation in local governance include the election of county commissioners and of county legislative councils and formation of citizens' development committees. In actual fact decisions are made at either state level or county level and passed for implementation without consultation with the grassroots.

3. **Centralized system of governance**: Since 2011 the government has been engaged in a process of 'recentralization' to create a strong executive model of government. This has seen many powers moved from states to the centre. In addition, states exercise considerable control over local governments, notably through the appointment of county commissioners and control of resources. At present the commissioners are appointed by the President of the Republic of South Sudan with the recommendation from the Governors of the States.

4. **Funds for services delivery**: Most of the funds are retained and spend at the central government level and some by the states and no adequate funds transferred to the counties for services delivery.

5. **Economic Crisis**: Drop in global oil prices greatly reduced oil revenue. The economic downturn was further exacerbated by the civil war. The collapse of Government revenues led to the board cutbacks, including centrally financed local government services. Again the situation has been made worse by deterioration in the exchange rate and high inflation. Although recently there is improvement in the exchange rate and non-oil revenue collection, still there is no any change realized in the economy.

6. **Qualified staff for local government**: At the local governments level there are no qualified staff that possess absorptive capacity to make plans for development. Every county commissioner when appointed, he/she appoint his/her own executive director and accountant to work with him/her. This had inflated the number of untrained redundant LGAOs and accountants who are not qualified.

7. **Lack of public participation and accountability**: Public participation and accountability provisions in the Local

Governmnent Act have generally not been realized in practice. Local governments also face significant capacity and resource constraints. Public perceptions of local governance effectiveness are weak.

8. **Civil wars**: The outbreak of civil war in December 2013 made the situation harder still. The deteriorating security situation made it difficult to access parts of the country, notably the conflict affected States of Unity, Jonglei and Upper Nile. Renewed fighting in July 2016 and the continuation of fighting by the hold out groups in the revitalized peace agreement and the Kit Gweng faction of the SPLM/A IO meant that the security continues to be an issue.

9. **Increasingly localized conflicts**: Following the economic collapse in 2012 and even more so after the outbreak of the civil war in December 2013, inter-and-intra-community fighting in South Sudan intensified. Local conflicts have also increasingly become part of the complex interconnected conflicts system. Some of the communities' conflicts persist in Jonglei, Warrap, Upper Nile and Central Equatoria States.

10. **Challenges brought about by creation of new states:** On April 17th 2016 the government increased the number of states from 10 to 28, with a further 4 added on 14th January 2017 making the total of South Sudan states to be 32. The move was seen as aimed at securing a balance of power in favour of the President's leadership and his supporters, strengthening patronage networks and undermining the opposition. There were fears it will lead to increased localized conflicts, and exacerbate the capacity and resource challenges already facing local governments. This has added to difficulties in the functioning of local governments for it has made the implementation of

local governance programmes harder. The new Counties created in 28 or 32 states did not benefit from the services which were being rendered by partners or NGOs who just kept on rendering services to the old Counties of former 10 States.

Moreover, the personnel and services that were already struggling to manage 10 states now were over stretched to cover three times that number. In addition, uncertainty about the future following the creation of new States demotivated public sector staff.

11. **Conflict over jurisdictions**: More new counties and municipalities were created during the creation of 28 and 32 states in 2016 and 2017 respectively. This brought conflicts over the jurisdictions which paralyzed their operations, particularly in revenue collection as exemplified by Tonj South County and Tonj Municipality in the defunct Tonj State.

12. **Conflict over the boundaries**: The Counties and Payams lack warrants of establishment this had caused some Payams to have conflicts over the boundaries.

13. **Corruption:** South Sudan languishes at the very bottom of international rankings measuring the perception of corruption and quality of government indicators. There is no political will to implement anti-corruption or transparency measures, and even if there was, it is questionable whether the country would have the necessary capacity to do so.

14. The country is vast and development efforts are concentrated in easy-to reach places. Donors hardly diversified aid to local levels. Urban areas have fared marginally better, with a huge amount of service delivery focused on Juba.

15. Funds for basic services have been disbursed unreliably to local government, hampering growing capacity where it matters most.

16. **Role of traditional authorities**: Chiefly institutions vary in structure and selection procedures in different areas of South Sudan. During colonial rule, the British adopted a system of native administration which entailed decentralization and use of traditional chiefs, notably for tax collection and conflict resolution. Traditional authorities continued to play that role after independence, including during the north-south civil war. They acted as intermediaries between communities and local governments. They were included in the system laid out in the 2009 LGA, though their role was not precisely defined. There are contradictions between modern values and traditional governance.

17. **Factors undermining chiefly authority**: A number of factors, mostly related to the civil war, have undermined traditional authorities in South Sudan. Displacement led to new chiefs emerging; government and armed forces also appointed new chiefs in areas that were under their control. Where traditional chiefs were retained, they were forced to do the bidding of armed groups/the government and faced severe punishments if they failed to do so. The 'humiliation' of traditional chiefs by armed forces, and the appointment of new chiefs, particularly the proliferation of appointments of chiefs during the creation of the 28 and 32 states, all combined weakened the chiefly authority.

18. **Effectiveness and legitimacy of state structures vs. traditional authorities**: While state local government structures enjoy legitimacy in law, provisions for these were laid down in the constitution and relevant legislation and their effectiveness was limited, and it was unclear how much public legitimacy they enjoyed. This is particularly given the lack of public participation in local governments. By contrast, traditional authorities

had in the past enjoyed both public legitimacy and had been seen as effective, particularly in conflict resolution. But their legitimacy had been undermined by the effects of the north-south civil war.

19. **Gender perspective and disabilities**: There was no literature looking at local governance in South Sudan specifically from the gender perspective or from that of people with disabilities.

20. **Role of the NGOs**: Most of the NGOs concentrated or replicated their services in certain particular areas of their choice and do not spread to all the counties and Payams in South Sudan which had contributed to marginalization of some counties.

12.3. Prospects for Local Government Administration in South Sudan

In order to let the local government administration prospers in South Sudan, the following need to be addressed vigorously:

1. Both the Constitution and the Local Government Act 2009 should be amended to suit the current situation.

2. The National Government to desist from the process of 'recentralization' and instead strengthen decentralization process or apply the system of federalism to devolve greater powers to the Local Government Administration.

3. Since there is no ministry of local government at the national level, Local Government Board should constitutionally be empowered to act as a clearing house for the central government for local affairs. It should be given the task of coordinating the work of all central departments' field administrations and of acting as the representative of the national government for the development and supervision of local government authorities in the country at large.

4. Commissioners and Councillors at all levels of local govern-
    ment administration should be elected to avoid the system of
    autocracy by the State Governors and County Commissioners.
5. Adequate funding of counties and Payams programmes has to be
    made so as to have quick impact on development at the local level.
6. All the units for service delivery should be established in all the
    Payams within the country.
7. Curtailment of the civil wars and eradication of communities'
    conflicts in order to sustain peaceful co-existence among the
    communities in the country.
8. Recruitment of local government administrative officers should
    be done either at the national level or state level and they should
    be university graduates and should first be given an induction
    course as in the past before deploying them to serve in the
    various counties and Payams in the country. The recruitment
    should be gender sensitive and inclusive of all the communities
    in the country before they are deployed to their states.
9. An academy of science for training local government administra-
    tive officers should be established by the Local Government Board
    or every state to establish its own training centre for LGAOs.
10. Recruitment of qualified supporting staffs in the Counties and
    Payams.
11. To halt the practice of every commissioner who appoint his/
    her own executive director and accountant.
12. The Local Government Board should coordinate with the
    states to prepare warrants of establishment of the Counties and
    Payams and resolve the issue of boundaries were disputes exist.
13. Desist from proliferation of creating many states, and if neces-
    sary, a scientific study should be carried out to consider differ-
    ent aspects of implications before creation of new states.

14. Zero-tolerance to corruption should not be a lip-service but be implemented drastically to deter people from corruption. Auditor general to audit every public organization to discover inappropriate malpractices and those who have made gross-misconducts be sued and convicted.

15. Provision of adequate transport means to every Payam to ease their operations. Every Payam should be provided with three vehicles: an ambulance, a truck and a Toyota land cruiser.

16. Both traditional authorities and local government officials should be helped to develop a clearer understanding of the links between county, state and central levels of government in order to be able to operate optimally within these new state structures.

17. The government should be supportive to work with traditional authorities.

18. To integrate traditional authorities and cultural values into states structures.

19. Traditional Authorities personnel should be paid salaries as in the past before 1983 war. Paramount Chiefs, Head Chiefs, Executive Chiefs, Sub-chiefs, Court Presidents, Court Members and Retainers were paid salaries. They were on the nominal rolls of the Rural Councils. Headmen or Gol Leaders were paid a commission of 2% from the collection of Social Service Tax they collect from the registered taxpayers of their clans.

20. Halls for Traditional Authorities Courts to be constructed instead of hearing cases under the trees.

21. National Government to construct all the roads connecting all the Payams in the Country and then equip Payams with equipments for roads repair.

22. LOGOSEED Programme should be extended to all the 79 counties in the country.
23. GIZ programme of water supply should be extended to at least the main towns in all the states of South Sudan.
24. NGOs should not be allowed to give services to areas of their choice but to be compelled to spread their services to all the different Payams of the country.

REFERENCES

Agere, Sam (2000). Promoting good governance. Commonwealth Secretariat. ISBN 978-0-85092-629-3. Found at Google Books.

Allister Hayman (6 October 2010). "LEPs: 22 bald men fighting over a comb?"

Al-Rodhan, Nayef R. F., *Sustainable History and the Dignity of Man: A Philosophy of History and Civilisational Triumph*, LIT, 2009.

An Act for the more easy assessing, collecting and levying of County Rates, (12 Geo. II c. 29).

Angry reaction to councils White Paper. The Times. October 8, 1983.

Anirban Kashyap: Panchaytiraj, Views of founding fathers and recommendation of different committees, New Delhi, Lancer Books, 1989.

"A User's Guide to Measuring Local Governance" UNDP.

Bennet, J. et al (2010). *Aiding the peace: a multi-donor evaluation of support to conflict prevention and peace building activities in southern Sudan 20015-2010.* ITAD, U.K. https://www.oecd.org/countries/southsudan/46895095.pdf.

Blackstone (1765).

Bridges Act 1803 (1803 c. 59) and Grand Jury Act 1833 (1833 c. 78).

Cape Getaway: Local Government Responsibilities.

Carl H. E. Zangerl, *The Social Composition of the County Magistracy in England and Wales, 1831–1887, The Journal of British Studies,* Vol. 11, No. 1. (November, 1971).

Carpenter, D. (2004). The Struggle for Mastery: Britain 1066-1284, Penguin History of Britain, London: Penguin, ISBN 0-14-014824-8.

Census data on population of Merthyr Tydfil.

Citizen Media Law Project: Identifying Federal, State, and Local Government Bodies.

Crozier, Michael P. (July 16, 2010). "Rethinking Systems". Administration & Society. **42** *(5): 504–525. doi: 10.1177/0095399710377443.*

Dally, M. W. Empire on the Nile: The Anglo-Egyptian Sudan 1898-9134. Cambridge University Press, Great Britain, 1986.

Dhal, A. Matoc, Local Government Financing in Southern Sudan, Khartoum University Press, Khartoum, Sudan, 2002.

Decentralization in India : Challenges and Opportunities, UNDP, 2000.

Department for Business, Innovation and Skills (7 September 2010). "New Local Enterprise Partnerships Criss-cross the Country". News Distribution Service. Retrieved 7 October 2010.

D. Lockard. The Politics of State and Local Government (2nd ed. 1969).

Eaton, Tim V., and Michael D. Akers. "Whistle Blowing and Good Governance". *CPA Journal* 77, no. 6 (June 2007): 66-71. *Business Source Complete*, EBSCO*host* (accessed March 22, 2016).

Elcock, H., *Local Government,* (1994).

E-TAPP (2016). *Lessons Learned: Developing PFM capacity to support basic service delivery in the fragile context of South Sudan.*

https://europa.eu/capacity4dev/eutapp/document/ eu-tapp-lessons-learned-brochure.

Fahim, Mayraj (24 May 2009). "Local government in India still carries characteristics of its colonial heritage". City Mayors Foundation.

File///c:/ASUS/Down loads/Local Governance in South Sudan_Overview_GSDRC.html. Iffat Idris, December 2018.

Fouéré, Marie-Aude. "*Julius Nyerere, Ujamaa, and Political Morality in Contemporary Tanzania.*" *African Studies Review 57.1 (2014): 1–24. Print.*

Foresti and Wild 2010. S "Support to political parties: a missing piece of the governance puzzle". London: Overseas Development Institute *Fukuyama, Francis (January 2013). "What Is Governance?" Center for Global Development. Working paper 314.*

German Cooperation, FACTSHEET, Torit Urban Water Supply and Sanitation Services Ltd. (TUWSS).

German Cooperation, FACTSHEET, Yambio Urban Water and Sanitation Services Company Ltd. (YUWASO).

German Cooperation, FACTSHEET, Yei Town Water and Sanitation Services Ltd. (YTWSS).

German Cooperation, Strengthening Local Governance and Resilience in South Sudan, Programme Outline 2016-2017.

GoSS and UNDP (2012). *South Sudan Recovery Fund (SSRF): Lessons Learned Exercise. Final Report.* Mptf.undp.org/document/ download/10126.

Government of India, Report of the Team for the Study of Community Projects and National Extension Service, (Chairperson: Balvantray Mehta), Committee on Plan Projects, National Development Council, (New Delhi, November 1957), Vol. I.

Grindle, Merilee (October 2004). "Good Enough Governance: Poverty Reduction and Reform in Developing Countries". Governance. **17** *(4): 525–48. Doi:10.1111/j.0952-1895.2004.00256.x.*

Henderson, K. D. D. The Making of Modern Sudan, Faber and Faber Limited, London, UK, 1953.

Her Majesty's Stationery Office, *Aspects of Britain: Local Government*, (1996).

Heritier, P. & Silvestri P. (Eds.), *Good government, Governance, Human complexity. Luigi Einaudi's legacy and contemporary societies*, Leo Olschki, Firenze, 2012H. Seeley, Local Government Explained @ Ivor H. Seeley, 1978.

"How Tuskegee Changed Research Practices". Center for Disease Control and Prevention, April 4, 2016.

http://documents.worldbank.org/curated/en/604951468739447676/pdf/multi-page.pdf.

Idris, I. (2017). *Local governance in South Sudan: overview.* K4D Helpdesk Report 235. Brighton, UK: Institute of Development Studies.

Idris, I. (2017). *Lessons from local governance programmes in South Sudan. K4D Helpdesk Report 236.* Brighton, UK: Institute of Development Studies.

J. J. Clarke, A History of Local Government of the United Kingdom (1985).

J. Richard Aronson and John L. Hilley, Financing State and Local Governments (Fourth Edition), the Brookings Institution, Washington, USA, 1986.

Kaufmann, Daniel and Kraay, Aart, "Growth Without Governance" (November 2002). World Bank Policy Research Working Paper No. 2928.

Khan, Mushtaq Husain (2004). State formation in Palestine: viability and governance during a social transformation: Volume 2 of Political economy of the Middle East and North Africa. Routledge. ISBN 978-0-415-33802-8. Found at Google Books.

Lal, Priya. "Militants, Mothers, and the National Family: Ujamaa, Gender, and Rural Development in Postcolonial Tanzania." The *Journal of African History 51.1 (2010): 1–20. Print 500.*

Larson, G. Ajak, P. & Pritchetl, L. (2013). *South Sudan's Capacity Trap: Building a State with Disruptive Innovation. Working Paper Series UNU-Wider Research Paper.* https://www.wider.unu.edu/sites/default/files/WP2013-120pdf.

Lawson, Robert (2012). "Book Review of Bo Rothstein: The quality of government: corruption, social trust, and inequality in international perspective". Public Choice. **150***(3–4): 793–795. doi:10.1007/s11127-011-9903-y.*

"Live blog: Sub-national economic growth white paper". 28 October 2010. Retrieved 28 October 2010.

"Local enterprise partnerships". Department of Communities and Local Government. 29 June 2010. Retrieved 7 October 2010.

Local Government Act 1972 (c.70), s.216.

Local Government Chronicle. Retrieved 7 October 2010.

Local government in England and Wales during the period of reconstruction (Cmd.6579).

LOGOSEED Documents.

London Gazette, May 1, 1935.

London Gazette, October 26, 1945.

Macnaghten, Phil; Owen, Richard (November 17, 2011). "Environmental science: Good governance for geo-engineering". Nature. **479** *(7373): 293. Bibcode:2011Natur. 479..293M. doi:10.1038/479293a. ISS N 00280836. PMID 22094673.*

Mahoj Rai et al. The state of Panchayats–A participatory perspective, New Delhi, Smscriti, 2001.

Mark Hoban (22 June 2010). *Budget 2010.* HM Treasury. Retrieved 7 October 2010.

Michela Giordano. Local Government in the United Kingdom. Internet.

Milestones in the Evolution of Local Government since Independence.

Mujeeb Muriana (2018). Who Creates Local Government and what are the Criteria for Local Government Creation in Nigeria, Munuich, GRIN Verlag, https://www.grin.com/document/962643.

Munshi, Surendra; Abraham, Biju Paul; Chaudhuri, Soma (March 12, 2009). The intelligent person's guide to good governance. New Delhi, India: Sage Publications. ISBN 9788178299310.

«National Council Of Educational Research And Training : Home». *www.ncert.nic.in. Retrieved 22 July 2019.*

N. Henry, Governing the Grass roots (3rd ed. 1987).

NORAD (2016). *South Sudan: Country Evaluation Brief.* https://www.norad.no/contentassets/8bbce9a79c8d4495a07de10caa2d-1dc/6.16_ceb_south_sudan.pdf.

Official website of State Election Commission.

Owens, Geoffrey Ross. "From Collective Villages to Private Ownership: Ujamaa, ." *Journal of Anthropological Research 70.2 (2014): 207–31. Print.*Tamaa, and the Postsocialist Transformation of Peri-Urban Dar Es Salaam, 1970–1990.

Oxfam (2015). *Six lessons from the Within and Without the State Governance Programme in South Sudan.* https://policy-practice.oxfam.org.uk/publications/six-lessons-from-the-within-and-without-thestate-programme-in-south-sudan-558452.

Phillips and Wetherell (1995).

Poluha, Eva; Rosendahl, Mona (2002). Contesting 'good' governance:crosscultural perspectives on representation, accountability and public space. *Routledge.* ISBN 978-0-7007-1494-0.

Pratiyogita Darpan. Pratiyogita Darpan. Retrieved 10 April 2015.

Quian, Yingyi (2003) 'How Reform Worked in China', in Rodrik.

R. D. Bingham, State and Local Government in an Urban Society (1986).

Redcliffe-Maud, Lord (1974). *English Local Government Reformed.* Wood, Bruce. Oxford University Press. ISBN 0-19-888091-X.

Regulation of Forces Act 1871.

Report of Local Government Board, January 2015.

Report of the Local Government Boundary Commission for the year 1947.

Report of the Royal Commission on the status of the County Borough of Merthyr Tydfil (Cmd.5039).

R. H. Leach and T. G. O' Rourke. State and Local Government, (1986).

Richard Rose; Caryn Peiffer (July 5, 2018). Bad Governance and Corruption. Springer. pp. 5–. ISBN 978-3-319-92846-3.

Rocha Menocal, A. (2011) "Analyzing the relationship between democracy and development", Overseas Development Institute.

*Rotberg, Robert (July 2014). "Good Governance Means Performance and Results". Governance. **27** (3): 511–518. doi:10.1111/gove.12084.*

Rothstein, Bo (2011). The quality of government: corruption, social trust, and inequality in international perspective. Chicago, IL: The University of Chicago Press.

Sheikheldin, Gussai H. "Ujamaa: Planning and Managing Development Schemes in Africa, Tanzania as a Case Study." Africology: The Journal of Pan African Studies 8.1 (2014): 78–96. Print.

Singh, Vijandra (2003). "Chapter 5: Panchayati Raj and Gandhi". Panchayati Raj and Village Development:Volume 3, Perspectives on Panchayati Raj Administration. Studies in public administration. New Delhi: Sarup & Sons. pp. 84–90. ISBN 978-81-7625-392-5.

Shourie, Arun (1990). *Individuals, institutions, processes: How one may strengthen the other in India today.* New Delhi, India:Viking.

S. Humes and E. martin, The Structure of Local Government (1969).

Soux, S. (2010). *Southern Sudan: Local governance in complex environments-project assessment.* UNDP. http://southsudanhumanitarianproject.com/wp-content/uploads/sites/21/formidable/soux-2010-Souther-Sudan-Local-Governance-in-Complex-Environments-Project -Assessment2.pdf.

"Take Five: "Elected Women Representatives are key agents for transformational economic, environmental and social change in India". UN Women. Retrieved 14 May 2020.

The Constitution (Seventy-third Amendment) Act, 1992.

The Constitution (Seventy Third Amendment) Act, 1992, The Gazette of India, Ministry of Law, Justice and Company Affairs, New Delhi, 1993.

The Constitution (Seventy-fourth Amendment) Act, 1992.

The Columbia Electronic Encyclopedia, 6th ed. Copyright © 2012, Columbia University Press.

"The Local Government System in India" (PDF). Commonwealth Local Government Forum.

The IMF and Good Governance", IMF. Accessed August 12, 2009.

«The IMF's Approach to Promoting Good Governance and Combating Corruption—A Guide». International Monetary Fund. June 20, 2005. Retrieved November 2, 2009.

T. M. Thomas Isaac with Richard Franke: Local democracy and development–Peoples Campaign for decentralized planning in Kerala, New Delhi, Left Word Books, 2000.

The Republic of South Sudan. LOGOSEED. Beneficiary Assessment of the Local Government and Service Delivery Project (LGSDP)-ID-127079, Final Report, November 2018.

The Republic of South Sudan. Ministry of Finance and Economic Planning and Local Government Board. Local Governance and Service Delivery Project, Credit No. 51230 and TF No. 018138. Financial Budget for the FY 2015/2016, Revised August 2015.

The Republic of South Sudan. Ministry of Finance and Planning and Local Government Board. Local Governance and Service Delivery Project. July 20 to June 2016, Annual Report, Abridged Version.

The Republic of South Sudan. Ministry of Finance and Economic Planning and Local Government Board. Local Governance and Service Delivery Project, Handover Notes, 29th November 2018.

The Republic of South Sudan. Office of the President. Local Government Board. Office of the Chairperson. Indicative Planning Figures for Fiscal Year 2017-18. Notice to State and County Officials and the General Public, 16 October 2017.

Tonj State, Tonj Municipality By-Laws, 2017.

UNDP (2016). *Country Programme Action Plan 2012-13.* http://www.ss.undp.org/content/dam/southsudan/library/Reports/southsudanotherdocuments/UNDP%20south%20sudan_CPA%202012-2013%20Fin%20siigned.pdf.

UNDP (2012). *Country Programme Document for the Republic of*

South Sudan July 2016-December 2017. http://www.ss.undp.org/content/dam/southsudan/library/Reports/southsudanotherdocuments/South%20Sudan%20CPD%20final_%July%202016%20to%20Dec%202017.pdf%20-%20Adobe%20Acrobat%20Pro.pdf.

"What is Good Governance". UNESCAP, 2009. Accessed April 6, 2021.

W. Blackstone. Commentaries on the Laws of England 339, 343 (1541).

Website on Decentralization and Local Governance in Kerala.

Wood, Bruce (1976). *The Process of Local Government Reform: 1966-1974.* George Allen & Unwin. ISBN 0-04-350052-8.

World Bank : Overview of rural decentralization.

World Bank: Overview of Rural Decentralization in India, Volume III, World Bank.

APPENDIX I

List of the names of the Ten States, names and numbers of the Counties, and number of Payams and Bomas in the Republic of South Sudan

S/No.	Name of the State	Name of the County	No. of Payams	No. of Bomas	Remarks
1	**Jonglei**	Bor	5	20	
		Twic East	5	20	
		Duk	4	16	
		Pibor★	5	20	★Pibor is now
		Pochalla	4	16	an administra-
		Akobo	7	28	tive area
		Nyirol	5	20	
		Wuror	5	20	
		Khorfulus	4	16	
		Fagak	5	20	
		Ayod	7	28	
	Sub-total	11	56	228	

2	Upper Nile	Baliet	10	20	
		Malakal	4	16	
		Manyo	4	16	
		Melut	4	16	
		Renk	5	32	
		Manyikang	4	16	
		Nasir	4	16	
		Longocuk	4	16	
		Ulang	4	55	
		Maiwut	6	24	
		Pacoda	5	25	
		Maban	12	48	
		Akoka	NA	NA	No records
	Sub-total	13	54	252	
3	Unity	Rupkona	4	16	
		Mayom	5	20	
		Leer	6	24	
		Panyijar	5	20	
		Mayendit	5	20	
		Pariang	4	16	★Abiemnhon
		Abiemnhom★	4	16	is now an
		Guit	4	16	administrative
		Kock	4	16	area
	Sub-total	9	37	164	

4	**Lakes**	Rumbek Central	6	NA	
			5	13	
		Rumbek North	7	NA	
			10	42	
		Rumbek East	7	22	
		Cueibet	4	12	
		Awerial	6	21	
		Wulu	6	14	
		Yirol West			
		Yirol East			
	Sub-total	8	51	124	
5	**Northern Bahr el Ghazal**	Awiel North	5	18	
		Awiel East	8	16	
		Awiel South	8	23	
		Awiel West	9	22	
		Awiel Centre	7	18	
	Sub-total	5	37	107	
6	**Warrap**	Twic	6	22	
		Gogrial East	6	18	
		Tonj East	6	22	
		Gogrial West	9	29	
		Tonj South	5	16	
		Tonj North	9	23	
	Sub-total	6	41	120	
7	**Western Bahr el Ghazal**	River Jur	6	24	
		Raja	7	28	
		Wau	5	20	
	Sub-total	3	18	72	

8	**Central Equatoria**	Lainya	5	14	
		Yei	4	16	
		Morobo	5	16	
		Kajokeji	5	31	
		Terekeka	8	43	
		Juba	14	111	
	Sub-total	6	41	231	
9	**Eastern Equatoria**	Kapoeta East	5	33	
		Kapoeta North	5	46	
			6	18	
		Lapon	7	26	
		Budi	5	24	
		Magwi	5	28	
		Kapoeta South	8	36	
		Torit	NA	NA	
		Ikotos			
	Sub-total	8	41	211	
10	**Western Equatoria**	Yambio	5	23	
		Mundri	5	17	
		Mundri West	4	13	
		Mundri East	5	19	
		Tombura	4	20	
		Ibba	5	13	
		Mvolo	7	24	
		Nzara	5	19	
		Ezo	6	25	
		Nagero	3	16	
	Sub-total	10	49	199	

	Grand Total	79		425	1,708	

Source: LOGOSEED Documents.

APPENDIX II

List of the names of the 28 States; names, numbers and headquarters of their Counties in South Sudan

Serial No.	Name of the State	Name of the County	Headquarters of the Counties
1	**Amadi**	Bangolo	Bangolo
		Karikyere	Karikyere
		Kedi'ba	Kedi'ba
		Mundri West	Mundri
		Mundri East	NA
		Mvolo	Mvolo
		Yeri	Yeri
		Witto	Jambo
	Sub-total	8	

2	**Awiel**	Bounchuai	Tiaraliet
		Kongdeir	Gagrol
		Ajak	Malek-Alel
		Barmayen	Barmayen
		Aroyo	Aroyo
		Ghiemel	Udhum
		Ajuet	Rum-Tiit
		Mayom Mel	Mayom-Mel
		Awiel Centre	Pan-Ameth Awiel
	Sub-total	9	
3	**Awiel East**	Malualbaai	Malual-Baai
		Madhol	Madhol
		Mangartong	Tiitchok
		War-Guet	Mareng
		Baac	Warawaar
		Wunlang	Rumakeer
		Mangok	Mangok
		Yargot	Yargot
	Sub-total	8	

4	**Eastern Bieh**	Alali	Alali
		Jokyier	Denjok
		Nyandid	Burmath
		Diror	Kalkuiny
		Walgak	Yidiit
		Pieri	Kuel Dhoal
		Padiek	Pateueat
		Weikol	Yohm
		Motdit	Pathal
		Pulchuol	Pulchuol
		Palker	Potot
		Waat	Waat
	Sub-total	12	
5	**Eastern Lakes**	Ngop	Ngop
		Aluakluak	Aluakluak
		Yirol	Yirol
		Abang	Abang
		Awerial South	Minkaman
		Awerial North	Bunagok
		Adior	Adior
		Lou	Nyang
	Sub-total	8	

6	**Eastern Nile**	Malakal	Malakal
		Renk	Renk
		Meluth	Meluth
		Baliet	Baliet
		Akoka	Akoka
		Mabam	Maban
		Koma	Dajo
		Khorfulus	Khorfulus
		Atar	Atar–Ardeba
	Sub-total	9	
7	**Fangak**	Fangak Central	Fangak Central
		Fangak North	Fangak North
		Fangak South	Fangak South
		Ayod Central	Ayod Central
		Ayod North	Ayod North
		Ayod South	Ayod South
	Sub-total	6	
8	**Gbudue**	Mupoi	Mupoi
		Ril	Ril
		Yubu	Yubu
		Naandi	Naandi
		Bangazogino	Bangazogino
		Basukangbi	Basukangbi
		Sakuru	Sakuru
		Bangasu	Bangasu
		Anzara	Anzara
		Ezo	Ezo
		Tombura	Tombura
		Nagero	Nagero
		Yambio	Yambio

		Sub-total	13	
9	**Gogrial**	Apuk North		Ntang-Jur
		Apuk West		Ajogo
		Apuk East		Lietnhom
		Apuk South		Pinydit
		Aguok North		Mayom Kadaduet
		Aguok West		Keet
		Awan Riau		Pan-liet
		Aguok Centre		Alek
		Awan Chan		Akon
		Awan Pajook		Mayen Pajook
		Aguok South		Gogrial Town
		Kuac North		Ajiep
		Kuac South		Karic
		Sub-total	13	
10	**Gok**	Cueibet		Cueibet
		Abiriu		Abiriu
		Duony		Malou
		Waat		Pagor
		Tiaptiap		Tiaptiap
		Malou Pec		Malou
		Sub-total	6	

11	**Imatong**	Torit	Torit
		Torit West	Kudo
		Torit East	Hiyala
		Lopa	Imehelek
		Lopit West	Longiro
		Lafon	Lafon
		Magwi	Magwi
		Ayaci	Ayaci
		Pageri	Pageri
		Ikwotos	Ikwoto
		Geria	Locomo
		Kidepo Valley	Chahari
	Sub-total	12	
12	**Jonglei**	Twic Centre	Twic Centre
		Twic South	Twic South
		Athooc	Athooch
		Anyidi	Anyidi Makuach
		Makuach	Kolnyan
		Kolnyan	Panyang
		Panyang	Duk Padiet
		Duk Padiet	Twic North
		Twic North	Duk Payuel
		Duk Payuel	
	Sub-total	9	
13	**Jubek**	Juba	NA
		Lokoya	NA
		Nyangwara	NA
	Sub-total	3	

14	**Latjor**	Thorow	Madding
		Malou	Kiechkuon
		Nasir	Nasir
		Ulang	Ulang
		Thior	Yomdong
		Longechuk	Mathiang
		Kaijak	Udier
		Maiwut	Maiwut
		Jekou	Pangak
	Sub-total	9	
15	**Lol**	Malual North	Gok Machar
		Malual Centre	Mapier Wieu
		Korok West	Juch
		Korok East	Maper Dut Thou
		Gumjuer East	Wed-Wiel
		Gumjuer West	Nyamlel
		Marial Baai	Marial Baai
		Majak Baai	Majak baai
		Kuru	Uyu-Kuku
		Ringi	Boro
		Ere	Ere
	Sub-total	11	
16	**Maridi**	Maridi	Maridi
		Ibba	Ibba
		Nabanga	Nabanga
		Mambe	Mambe
		Kozi	Kozi
	Sub-total	5	

17	**Northern Lich**	Mayom	NA
		Koch	NA
		Rubkona	NA
		Guit	NA
	Sub-total	4	
18	**Namurnyang**	Kapoeta South	Kapoeta
		Kapoeta North	Nasikal
		Kapoeta East	Narus
		Budi	Chukudum
		Kuato	Nanyangacor
		Kimotong	Napaka
		Timo	Dongsike
		Ngawuro	Ngawuro
	Sub-total	8	
19	**Boma**	Pochala	NA
		Pibor	NA
	Sub-total	2	
20	**Ruweng**	Abiemnhom South	Abiemnhom
		Abiemnhom North	Awarpiny
		Panrieng North	Panyang
		Panrieng East	Jamjang
		Panrieng South	Biu
	Sub-total	5	

21	**Southern Liech**	Thornyor	Thornyor
		Bou	Bou
		Dhorwang	Dhorwang
		Mayendit	Mayendit
		Rubkuai	Rubkuai
		Tharjiathbor	Tharjiathbor
		Panyijar	Panyijar
		Ganyiil	Ganyiil
		Nyaal	Nyaal
	Sub-total	9	
22	**Terekeka**	Gemeiza	Gemeiza
		Gwoe	Bura
		Tali	Tali
		Terekeka	Terekeka
		Terekeka North	Ral
		Tijor	Tijor
		Nyori	Gwongoro
	Sub-total	7	

23	**Tonj**	Luanyjang South	Makuac
		Luanyjang Centre	Romic
			Pagor
		Luanyjang North	Paweng
			Wunlit
		Lunayjang East	Ngapagok
		Jalwau	Palal
		Ngapagok★	Thiet
		Palal★	Wanhalel
		Thiet	Mabior Yar
		Wanhalel	Jak
		Mabior Yar★	Tonj
		Jak	Manyangok
		Tonj	Alabek
		Manyangok	Aliek
		Alabek	Akop
		Aliek	Rualbet
		Akop	Marial Lou
		Rualbet	Pagol
		Marial Lou★	Kirik
		Pagol	Awuul
		Kirik	Majak
		Awuul★	Warrap
		Majak	Manloor
		Warrap	
		Manloor	
	Sub-total	24	
24	Tombura	Tombura	Tombura
		Nagero	Nagero

		Sub-total	2w	
25	**Twic**	Ajak	Ajak Kuac	
		Aweng	Aweng	
		Turalei	Turalei	
		Wunrok	Wunrok	
		Pan-Nyok	Pan-Nyok	
		Akoc	Akoc	
		Sub-total	6	
26	**Western Lakes**	Eastern Bahr	Akot/Dual	
		Naam	Rumbek	
		Rumbek	Pacong	
		Western Bahr	Wulu	
		Naam	Meen	
		Wulu	Malek	
		Malueth	Maper	
		Malek	Bahr El Ghel	
		Alor	Pagang	
		Bahr El Gel		
		Pagang		
		Sub-total	9	
27	**Western Nile**	Panyikang	Atigo	
		Pachoda	Kodok	
		Manyo	Wodakona	
		Atulpi	Doleib Hill	
		Wij Reg	Lul	
		Akurwa	Kaka	
		Nyilua	Pakwar	
		Sub-total	7	

28	**Yei River**	Kajokeji	Kajokeji
		Lainya	Lainya
		Yei	Yei
		Kupera	Kupera
		Kindi	Kindi
		(Morobo) East	Udabi
		Kindi	Gaderu
		(Morobo) West	Tore
		Nyepo	Otogo
		Tore	
		Otogo	
	Sub-total	9	
	Grand Total	233	

Source:

Republican Order No. 13/2016 for the Creation of New Counties in Twenty Eight (28) States in the Decentralized System of Government in the Republic of South Sudan, 2016 A. D. dated April 17th, 2016. Pp. 2-13.

Note: Data on some counties of some states is not available.
★Counties that got created afterwards.

APPENDIX III

List of the names and capitals of 32 States; names and numbers of their Counties; in the Republic of South Sudan

S/No.	Name of the State	Counties of the State	Capital of the State
1	Gogrial	Apuk North Apuk West Apuk East Apuk South Aguok North Aguok West Awan Riau Aguok Centre Awan Chan Awan Pajook Aguok South Kuac North Kuac South	Kuajok
	Sub-total	13	

5	Western Lakes	Rumbek North Rumbek Centre Wulu Akot Paloc Western Bahr Naam Amongpiny Malek Bahr Gel Aloor Malueth Eastern Bahr Naam	Rumbek
	Sub-total	12	
6	Eastern Lakes	Yirol East Yirol Centre Awerial East Anuol Gar Aluakluak Malek Nyang Awerial South Awerial North Awerial Centre Geng Geng Abang Ngop Yali	Yirol

	Sub-total	15	
7	Aweil East	Malualbaai Madhol Mangartong War–Guet Baac Wunlang Mangok Yargot	Wanjok
	Sub-total	8	
8	Lol	Malual North Malual Centre Korok West Korok East Gumjuer East Gumjuer West Marial Baai Majak Baai Kuru Ringi Ere	Raja
	Sub-total	9	

9	Aweil	Aweil Centre	Aweil
		Bounchuai	
		Kongdeir	
		Ajak	
		Barmayen	
		Aroyo	
		Ghiemel	
		Ajuet	
		Mayom Mel	
	Sub-total	9	
10	Wau	Kuarjiena	Wau
		Rocrocdong	
		Marial Bai	
		Udici	
		Kangi	
		Besselia	
		Bagari	
		Kpaile	

11	Jubek	Lodu	Juba
		Luri	
		Mangala	
		Gondokoro	
		Rejaf	
		Wonduruba	
		Lobonok	
		Bungu	
		Ganji	
		Ganzi	
		Dollo	
		Rokon	
		Liriya	
		Oponi	
	Sub-total	14	
12	Terekeka	Terekeka North	Terekeka
		Terekeka South	
		Jemeiza	
		Gwor	
		Tali	
		Tijor	
		Nyori	
	Sub-total	7	

13	Yei River	Yei	Yei
		Lainya	
		Morobo	
		Kajokeji	
		Kupera	
		Kindi (Morobo) East	
		Kindi (Morobo) West	
		Nyepo	
		Tore	
		Otogo	
	Sub-total	10	
14	Tombura	Tombura	Tambura
		Ezo	
		Nagero	
		Mupoi	
		Naandi	
		Yangiri	
		Source Yubu	
	Sub-total	7	
15	Gbudwe	Yambio	Yambio
		Anzara	
		Basukangbi	
		Nadiangre	
		Sakura	
		Bangasu	
		Bazangazagino	
	Sub-total	7	

16	Amadi	Mundri West Mundri East Bangolo Karikyere Kedi'ba Mvolo Yeri Witto	Mundri
	Sub-total	8	
17	Maridi	Maridi Ibba Nabanga Mambe Kozi	Maridi
	Sub-total	5	
18	Imatong	Lopa Torit Ikotos Magwi Torit West Torit East Lopit West Lafon Magwi Ayasi Pageri Ikwotos Geria Kidepo Valley	Torit
	Sub-total	14	

19		Kapoeta North	Kapoeta
		Kapoeta East	
		Kapoeta South	
		Budi	
		Kuato	
		Kimotong	
		Timo	
		Ngawuro	
20	Jonglei	Twic Centre	Bor
		Twic South	
		Athooc	
		Anyidi Makuach	
		Kolnyan	
		Panyang	
		Duk Padiet	
		Twic North	
		Duk Payuel	
	Sub-total	9	
21	Fangak	Fangak Central	Ayod
		Fangak North	
		Fangak South	
		Ayod Central	
		Ayod North	
		Ayod South	
	Sub-total	6	

22	Bieh (Uror and Nyirol)	Majok Pultruk Padding Dini Padiek Muudit Pulchuol Pathati Wichkol Palker Peiri	Waat
	Sub-total	10	
23	Akobo	Alali Dengjok Nyandit Diror Walgak	Akobo
	Sub-total	5	
24	Maiwut	Longuchuk Koma Maiwut	Maiwut
	Sub-total	3	
25	Latjor	Ulang Nasir Malou Gawang Wanding Dome Yomding Kawat	Nasir
	Sub-total	8	

26	Boma	Pochalla Pibor	Pibor
	Sub-total	2	
27	Central Upper Nile	Malakal Akoka Pigi Baliet Panyikang	Malakal
	Sub-total	5	
28	Northern Upper Nile	Renk Maban Melut	Renk
	Sub-total	3	
29	Fashoda	Kodok Manyo	Kodok
	Sub-total	2	
30	Ruweng	Abiemnhom South Abiemnhom North Panrieng North Panrieng East Panrieng South	Panraing
	Sub-total	5	

31	Southern Liech	Mayendit Leer Thornyor Bou Dhorwang Rubkuai Tharjiath Panyijar Ganyliel Nyaal	Leer
	Sub-total	10	
32	Northern Liech	Mayom Koch Rubkona Guit	Bentiu
	Sub-total	4	
	Grand Total	295	

Sources:

1. Republican Order No. 13/16 for the Creation of New Counties in the Twenty Eight (28) States in the Decentralized System of Government in the Republic of South Sudan, 2016 A.D. dated April 17th, 2016.

2. Republican Order No. 02/2017 for the Creation of new States in the Republic of South Sudan, 2017 A.D. of 14th January 2017.

3. Republic of South Sudan, Office of the President, The Local Government Board, Office of the Chairperson, Correction of the Counties of Jonglei State (12), dated 5th September, 2016.

4. Interviews with Hon. Madhang Majok Meen, former Governor of Gok State; Hon. Job Alawei Magot, Commissioner of Awerial North County, Eastern Lakes State Hon. Tombura Tut Jal, former Minister of Agriculture, Forestry, Fisheries and Livestock, Latjor State.

★ *Counties that got created afterwards.*

Index

France vii, 12, 17, 69-73, 75-6
Francis 112-113, 257
French Sta, 70-3, 79
Fukuyama 112-113, 257
Gaafar 126
Gabriel xvi, 236
Gagrol 273
Galobawi 125, 131-2
Gandhi 93
Ganyiil 282
Garang xvi, 138
Gauteng 62
Gbudue 276
Gemeiza 283
Genanyuon 237-238
Gender 169, 184, 249, 258
Geo 255
Geoffrey 260
George 130, 264
Geria 278
German xii, xxi, 174, 182, 192, 226-7, 229-231, 257
Ghazal 143, 192, 210-1, 213, 215, 217-8, 220, 222, 268
Ghiemel 273
Gibana 160
Gildenhuys 33-35
Giordano 77, 81, 87, 259
Globalization v, 58-9
Gogrial 195-196, 200, 202-3,

211, 214, 218, 221, 237, 268, 277
Gok xvi, 277, 280
Gol 253
Gomme 9, 13
Governance lev, xii, xxv, 97, 99-100, 102-3, 105, 110, 112-6, 119-121, 175, 177-8, 182, 185, 187, 189-190, 192, 195-6, 202, 206-7, 227, 229, 256-7, 260-4
Governmnent 246
Gram 94
Grindle, Merilee. 113, 257
Guit 210, 214, 217, 220, 267, 281
Gumjuer 280
Gussai 261
Gweng 247
Gwoe 283
Gwongoro 283
Hakuma 4
Halved 92
Hampshire 115
Handover 263
Hart 19
Hassan 92
Hayman, A. 255
Headmanship 166
Headmanships 166
Headmen 253